DRIVING EMERGENCIES

DRIVING EMERGENCIES

JAMES JOSEPH

**and the Editors of
Consumer Reports Books**

CONSUMER REPORTS BOOKS
A Division of Consumers Union
Yonkers, New York

Copyright © 1994 by James Joseph and
Consumers Union of United States, Inc., Yonkers, New York 10703.

Published by Consumers Union of United States, Inc.,
Yonkers, New York 10703.

Library of Congress Cataloging-in-Publication Data

Joseph, James, 1924–
    Driving emergencies / James Joseph and the editors of Consumer
Reports Books.
      p. cm.
    Includes index.
    ISBN 0-89043-681-9
    1. Automobile driving—Safety measures. 2. Automobiles—
Maintenance and repair—Miscellanea. I. Consumer Reports Books.
II. Title.
TL152.5.J667   1994
629.28'3—dc20   93-48002
                                                  CIP

All photographs and art by James Joseph, except
page 21 (courtesy of National Oceanic and Atmospheric Administration)
and page 58 (courtesy of California Division of Highways).

Design by GDS/Jeffrey L. Ward

First printing, May 1994

This book is printed on recycled paper.

Manufactured in the United States of America

Driving Emergencies is a Consumer Reports Book published by Consumers Union, the nonprofit organization that publishes *Consumer Reports*, the monthly magazine of test reports, product Ratings, and buying guidance. Established in 1936, Consumers Union is chartered under the Not-for-Profit Corporation Law of the State of New York.

    The purposes of Consumers Union, as stated in its charter, are to provide consumers with information and counsel on consumer goods and services, to give information on all matters relating to the expenditure of the family income, and to initiate and to cooperate with individual and group efforts seeking to create and maintain decent living standards.

    Consumers Union derives its income solely from the sale of *Consumer Reports* and other publications. In addition, expenses of occasional public service efforts may be met, in part, by nonrestrictive, noncommercial contributions, grants, and fees. Consumers Union accepts no advertising or product samples and is not beholden in any way to any commercial interest. Its Ratings and reports are solely for the use of the readers of its publications. Neither the Ratings, nor the reports, nor any Consumers Union publications, including this book, may be used in advertising or for any commercial purpose. Consumers Union will take all steps open to it to prevent such uses of its material, its name, or the name of *Consumer Reports*.

CONTENTS

PART 3. MECHANICAL EMERGENCIES

DRIVING EMERGENCIES

INTRODUCTION

This book can tell you how to meet and extricate yourself from virtually any driving emergency you will ever face. It is meant to be consulted not simply when you need help but also in anticipation of the kinds of emergencies every driver should be prepared for.

Its chapters detail many of the driving, electrical, mechanical, weather, and personal emergencies you are likely to encounter while on the road, in town, or as close to home as your own driveway.

This book can tell you what to do if the gas pedal jams, if the brakes suddenly fail, if the power steering quits, or if an instrument panel alert suddenly comes on. Also, it gives advice to drivers who may face a sudden windstorm, a flash flood, a smashed or opaqued windshield, an engine fire, a drunk driver, a front-tire blowout, and other driving emergencies.

In general, this book's emergency solutions do not require many tools, nor any real mechanical knowledge. It is recommended, however, that all drivers assemble and travel with an emergency kit similar to the one described in this book (see Car Emergency Kit below).

➤ CAR EMERGENCY KIT

Here's a car emergency kit that's easily put together at modest cost. It contains items that can extricate you and your car from many of the emergency situations detailed in this book.

Emergency kit component	Typical uses
1. Spare tire*	Replaces flat or ruined tire
2. Tire-changing jack*	For changing a tire; other emergency uses
3. Tire-changing tool(s)*	For tire/wheel changing
4. Tire chains (pair fitted for your car's wheels)	To control car on icy, snowy pavement; increase traction if mired in mud, sand, snow
5. Screwdrivers (slotted and Phillips)	For tightening, prying, etc.
6. Wire (50 feet, 20 gauge, easy to bend, easy to twist-tie)	To tie down hood, secure tailpipe and muffler, etc.

*Standard equipment in most cars

7. Duct (cloth) tape (30 feet, 2 inches wide) — Temporarily stops leaks in most cars; all-purpose taping

8. Scissors, knife, or utility knife — For cutting duct tape, light-gauge wire, hoses, belts

9. Fuel/water container (1 gallon, plastic, with flexible nozzle) — For gasoline, water

10. Funnel (metal or plastic) — For filling gas tank, water, oil, etc.

11. Adjustable wrench, vise-type pliers — For bolt-head fasteners, connections

12. Siphon kit — To siphon gas

13. Rags/paper towels — For handling hot engine parts

14. Aerosol lubricant — To unstick door locks; all-purpose lubricating

15. Motor oil (resealable quart size) — Replenish oil

16. Shovel, trowel, or trenching tool — To clear away snow, mud, sand, and restore wheel traction

17. Large, sturdy flashlight — For nighttime emergencies

18. Fire extinguisher (40 ounce, dry type) — For car fire (grease, oil, electrical)

19. Jumper cables (pair, 12 feet long) — For jump-starting car battery

20. Rope (25 feet, minimum, ⅜-inch diameter) — Various uses

21. 2 flares (each approx. 15 minutes duration) — Road distress signal (day or night)

22. Squirt bottle (pint size with squirt dispenser) — For cooling engine's fuel, other liquids lines; and for other uses

23. Hammer or hatchet-hammer combination — To cut small tree limbs, underbrush for tread traction (if stuck in mud, snow, sand)

24. First-aid kit — For medical emergencies

PART 1

NATURE- OR WEATHER-RELATED EMERGENCIES

SURVIVE IF BURIED IN AN AVALANCHE

Driving along a snowy, high-country road, you hear an avalanche alert on the radio. The road you're driving on is lined with snow slopes. Then suddenly, without warning, without even the rumble you might have expected, it happens: the world around you whites out. Tons of snow stop your car dead. Under the hood, the hot engine steams and hisses as cold snow seeps over it. The car radio goes silent, its antenna buried. In the eerie moments that follow, a stolid solitude settles around you.

➤ WHAT TO DO

1. Shut off the engine immediately, if it isn't stopped already. Your immediate danger is carbon monoxide poisoning, not freezing or suffocating. With the tailpipe buried, there's no escape for the engine's exhaust. If you leave the engine on, carbon monoxide can overcome you in minutes.
2. Stifle panic and think your situation through. Buried in your car on a public road, you're far luckier than if you were caught on the open slopes. Road crews, probably already alerted to a slide blocking the road, should shortly be on their way with heavy equipment.
3. You can stay in the car, keep as warm as possible, and await rescue. For most, this may be the wisest choice. You can bundle up in a coat for warmth. Temporarily, you should have enough air.
4. If you can, thrust something to the surface to pinpoint your position to rescuers. Metal ceiling moldings, or even straightened seat springs with their sections overlapped and bound with tape stripped from wiring under the instrument panel, may serve as a flagpole to which you can tie a bright piece of cloth.
5. Or you may choose—depending on the car's position (upright or on its side) and whether it is daylight or nighttime—to attempt an escape. Escape is easier if the car is upright (opening a window won't inundate the car's interior with snow), and you try it in daylight. If light shows through the snow, you may be buried only a few feet.
6. Before you attempt to escape, dress as warmly as you can. Buckle your coat securely and snugly to streamline your body. Cover your face with a makeshift bandanna.

5

Ungroomed, snowy slopes can avalanche over a road without warning.

Create snowshoes by cutting up clothing, the car's seats, or upholstery. Wrap the material around your ankles and shoes and tie it securely. Where shoes would slip through the snow, snowshoes should give you footing for climbing. Wear gloves if you have them (they are better for shoveling snow than bare hands) or cover your hands with extra socks, rags, towels, etc.

7. When you're ready to go, open a side window (assuming the car is upright) just wide enough to slide through. If you have power windows they, like the car's battery, should still be working.

8. Once out of the car, begin "swimming" to the surface using a breaststrokelike motion (move your arms out, then draw them toward you), keeping as large a breathing area ahead of you as possible. As you advance toward the surface, your snowshoes should prevent you from slipping back.

SURVIVE A SUDDEN BLIZZARD

You heard the warnings on the car radio. Suddenly, what has been threatening to strike for hours does: one of those headline-making blizzards. Its 60-mph wind-blown snow whites out everything more than a few feet ahead, behind, and around you.

Quickly, the windshield wipers become useless, unable to push aside the snow accumulating on the glass and blanketing the hood. The defoggers do nothing. A curtain of gusting snow all but extinguishes the reach of your headlights. You can't make out the headlights of approaching cars until they are virtually upon you, and vice versa.

Whether on a main city street or on the highway, you are isolated, alone, trapped. Yet, for the moment at least, you are protected by your car. As your breath fogs and opaques the windows and windshield, the cold and reality set in.

In a blizzard, quickly switch on the wipers and decide whether to seek shelter.

7

For many drivers, it is a moment of fear, perhaps even terror. Every winter hundreds of motorists are similarly trapped, stranded in their snow-covered cars on the highway or on city streets.

➤ WHAT TO DO

Before setting out when a blizzard is threatening:

1. Phone the local weather bureau, the highway patrol, or sheriff's office for predictions of road conditions over the route you plan to drive. If you hear only a recorded blizzard forecast—which may be hours old—phone a local newscaster for the latest weather advisory.
2. If the report is ominous, stay wherever you are—at home, in a motel, even at work.

If caught on the road before the blizzard's full fury strikes:

1. Tune to a local radio station to learn of the storm's progress.
2. If winds increase and snowfall turns heavy, carefully gauge the road's visibility and snow depth.
3. If the snow is deeper than a few inches (the crunching sound of your tires treading through the snow will tell you), do what most drivers are loath to do: retreat. Stifle your natural tendency to press on.

     Quickly find a safe place to turn and head back. Turning back, you may outrun the storm or elude the worst of it (depending on the direction of the storm). Often, you'll find the road and visibility surprisingly clear once you've retreated. Retracing your route has another lifesaving advantage. Rather than pressing on into the unknown, you'll be driving a familiar route. You'll know where the potential shelters are because you passed them—service stations, restaurants, motels, even farm or ranch houses.
4. If, in turning back, you don't outrun or elude the storm, immediately get off the highway and into shelter. Don't make the mistake of pressing on even a mile farther, hoping the storm will abate. If it does, you can always take to the road again. For the moment, get to a shelter. Blizzards can block highways and their escape roads in minutes.

If bogged down in a blizzard:

1. Stay in your car.
2. Don't risk venturing out into the biting winds and blinding snow except, perhaps, to

tie something colorful—a sock, panty hose, rag, scarf—to the car's antenna so that snowplow crews and police can spot your car if it becomes buried. If the antenna isn't at maximum height, raise it.

3. Don't fool yourself into believing that you can walk to shelter, even if you know it's only a block or even a few hundred yards away. If you venture even a few feet from your car in the worst of blizzards, you risk becoming lost (often you can't see a hand's distance ahead).

4. Look to your survival. Blizzard-trapped drivers have reported making extraordinary efforts to stay warm: wrapping themselves in seat covers, cutting seat cushions or floor mats into insulating pads (slipped into shirts and blouses), and exercising between short runs of the car's heater. Keeping the engine running risks carbon monoxide poisoning (exhaust fumes trapped beneath the chassis can seep upward into the passenger compartment) and emptying your fuel tank. Running your engine overnight can use six to eight gallons of gasoline. It's better and safer to accelerate the engine to high idle (just fast enough for the battery gauge or indicator to show that the battery is being charged) for 15 minutes every hour with at least one window cracked open a few inches. During that same period you can try to use the heater. But the snow-packed radiator, robbed of its usual heat-exchange medium—air— may overheat and deprive you of even brief use of the heater. And in the fiercest of blizzards, melted snow in the engine compartment can short out the ignition system, killing the engine and making a restart impossible.

5. Refrain from drinking alcoholic beverages. Their immediate warming effect is illusionary. Alcohol opens the skin's pores, robbing the body of heat and dangerously increasing body chill. No matter how thirsty you get, don't eat snow. Melt it first— use a match to warm the underside of a snow-filled ashtray or hold any makeshift container up to a heater outlet. Raw snow causes blood to rush to the stomach, chilling the body's extremities and its already-cooling blood supply.

6. Wait for rescuers. They'll arrive in time. Most blizzard-area rescue teams have snowmobiles or can get them when necessary.

DEICE A WINDSHIELD

If you drive in cold weather, chances are it has happened to you: the windshield has iced over. And not just a paper-thin layer of the cold stuff, but an overnight buildup from sleet or wet snow that quick-freezes to the glass—thick layers of ice that opaque the windshield. Is it an emergency? It is if you need to get somewhere in a hurry.

The defrosters are the windshield deicers of first choice. If you have a plastic ice scraper (or a handy substitute device), use that as well. Of course, the best way to beat ice on the windshield is by taking preventive measures. The night before a snowfall or freezing rain, cover the windshield with plastic wrap, wax paper, cardboard, a tarp, or a blanket. Come morning, all you need to do is lift the material off and the ice lifts off, too. But a sudden freeze may catch motorists unprepared.

➤ WHAT TO DO

1. Start the engine. As on most cold mornings, start the engine before turning on any car electrical accessories. You need maximum battery cranking power for cold-starting.
2. With the engine started and warming, switch on the windshield defrosters. In this quick-defrost scenario, the defrosters work on the ice from the inside of the car while you attack from outside the car. (Use no tools or chemicals that might scratch the windshield's glass or damage the car's finish.)
3. Set to work with the tools you have: a plastic ice scraper (or substitute device), a hair dryer plugged into the dashboard's cigarette lighter or powered by an extension cord from a house or garage electrical outlet, and a screwdriver (with its cutting edge wrapped so it can't scratch the glass) to help break the ice.
4. The deicing job can often be speeded up by splashing some windshield washer anti-freeze solution on the ice. If the windshield fluid container under the hood lifts out, or if you can siphon some out into a handy container, simply pour the antifreeze directly onto the ice.

GET STARTED ON A SUPER-ICY DRIVEWAY

The name of the game when driving on ice is traction. Tires need to grip something—whether on ice or snow, or on a wet and slippery pavement—to get you moving. How well tires bite into a slippery surface is a measure of traction.

On icy, slippery driveways you may not have enough traction, even if your car has snow or studded tires. A car is simply not designed to drive on ice. But after a wet snowfall or sleet, followed by a quick freeze, your driveway may become an ice rink. With a steep or curved driveway, you risk fishtailing the rear of your car into a tree, a fence, or even the house. Escaping the driveway can be almost as perilous as driving on a slippery street.

Although the tedious job of putting on tire chains will probably solve your driveway traction problem, there are easier, less time-consuming ways to get the traction the tires need to maneuver on ice.

To get traction, you need to put something between the ice and the tires' treads. Deflating the tires will not provide better traction. Nor will accelerating in the vain hope that somehow the fast-spinning wheels will bite into the ice and get the car moving.

➤ WHAT TO DO

1. Try shoveling the snow (easier if it's dry and crunchy) ahead of the drive wheels. If that doesn't work, try adding something more abrasive to the road: sand, gravel, dirt. Narrow-width boards laid parallel and a few inches apart ahead of the drive wheels may get you going. Pieces of carpeting, cardboard, even the tire chains themselves (spread just ahead of the drive tires, rather than fitted to them) may work. But if you use chains this way, have any bystanders move well clear of the car, especially from behind it, because anything placed beneath the tires can be thrown about if the tires grip unevenly. Due to the risk of injury, having someone push you off a slippery patch of ice (with or without the use of chains) should be avoided.

   If the driveway is slick all the way to the street, you may have to lay your traction material at least that far.
2. With traction material in place, start the engine. Put the transmission in *highest* gear

11

(in Drive for automatic cars, third or higher gear for standard shifts). The reason for this is you want to apply the least amount of torque—power—to the wheels.

3. With the transmission in highest gear, very gently apply a *little* power with the gas pedal. Too much power can cause the tires to spin even with gravel, snow, or traction material laid beneath them. Another way to ease the power with a standard shift is to slip the clutch.

4. As the car begins to move, steer carefully down the slippery drive. Be aware that, unless you've laid a path of traction, the wheels may lose their grip before you reach the street. Therefore, ease up on the gas pedal and keep the gear in high.

5. Once the car is in motion, keep it moving. Don't stop. Don't suddenly accelerate, either. Simply keep the tires rolling.

OPEN A FROZEN OR STUCK DOOR LOCK

On a frigid morning you try to insert your key in the car door lock. It won't fit. Or, if the key does fit, it won't turn in the lock. Something has suddenly gone wrong with the lock. Maybe. More likely, the lock is rusted or stuck.

Moisture may have gotten into the lock and frozen overnight, or the lock may have been lubricated improperly, perhaps with regular lubricating oil or a dry graphite. Although both lubricants are commonly used for interior locks, they should not be used to lubricate exterior locks. Both tend to gum up the works.

The proper lubricant for exterior car locks is a chemically modified, although petroleum-based, lubricant that works quite differently than lubricating oil, which can thicken and freeze

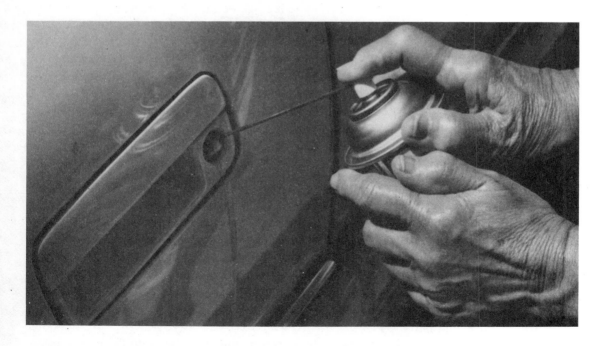

A squirt of lubricant in a stuck or frozen lock will often free it.

in especially cold weather. Chemical/petroleum-based lubricants are available at most auto supply and hardware stores.

Whatever the cause for the failure, you are locked out just as surely as if you had lost the key.

➤ WHAT TO DO

When a car door lock is frozen:

1. Try the other doors. Their locks may not be frozen. It's surprising how many drivers, frozen out of their cars, never think to try the car's other doors.
2. If all the doors are frozen, get an aerosol spray can of the chemically modified lubricant and squirt some into the frozen lock's keyhole.

   Some aerosol lubricants come with a little plastic tube that lets you direct the lubricant deep into the lock. Insert the tube as far into the lock as it will go and give the lock a good dose of lubricant. Let the lubricant penetrate the lock mechanism. This may take a few minutes.

   With the lock lubricated, spray some lubricant on the key, insert the key in the lock, and gently turn the key left and right. This may be enough to get the lock working. If not, repeat the process several times.
3. If it's still frozen, try any of several other means: try heating the key. To prevent burning your fingers, hold the key in a gloved hand, in the jaws of a vise grip or common pliers, or, if you have nothing else handy, a folded handkerchief or a rag.

   Heat the key with a match or, better, with a cigarette lighter or candle. When the key is hot, insert it in the lock. Count to five and try to turn the key. (Turn the key gently to test thawing and to prevent breaking the key.) If it still won't turn in the lock, reheat the key and try again. Thawing occurs gradually and may require repeated tries. If the lock is frozen, repeated applications of the warmed key should get the lock working.

   You might try heating the lock with a hair dryer. Use an extension cord long enough to plug into a convenient electrical outlet. Then hold the dryer as close to the lock as possible to avoid heating the car's surrounding finish.

   Another tactic is to squirt a deicing fluid (like antifreeze from the radiator or from the windshield fluid container) into the lock. Siphon the antifreeze into a squirt bottle or use a commercial deicing chemical available at most auto supply stores. Commercial deicers come in tubes. Insert the tube's nozzle into the keyhole and squeeze the fluid into the lock.
4. After you've thawed and opened the lock, squirt some lubricant into the lock. The lubricant will drive moisture from the lock mechanism and prevent refreezing.

When a car door lock is stuck:

1. Squirt the lubricant into the lock. Gently turn the key. If the lock is still stuck, repeat. Usually several applications of the lubricant will free the mechanism—even if it's rusted.
2. Whether it's frozen or simply stuck, and if you don't have a chemically modified type of lubricant, use any light oil or dry graphite. Later, you can flush them out of the lock with the lubricant. Your objective, ideal lubricant or not, is to unlock the door and get on your way.

GET OUT OF A SNOWBANK

If you leave the car out all night and heavy snows bury it, or if you accidentally back into a pile of snow while turning around on a snowy road, or unexpectedly skid into snow, you may find yourself stuck in a snowbank. However you get there, you need to know how to get your car out.

➤ WHAT TO DO

1. Carefully survey your predicament. Will a little shoveling clear the way for the drive wheels to power you free, or does ice beneath the tires compound the problem? Is the snow so slushy that the drive wheels will just dig deeper if you attempt to drive out, or is the snow dry enough for the treads to grip onto?

2. If you carry tire chains, getting free can be as quick and easy as spreading a chain ahead of each drive wheel and slowly driving out over your ''chain road.'' But have your passengers stand well away from the car: the wheels may throw the chains when you apply power.

3. Without chains, you may have to dig the tires free using a shovel or a trowel. If you don't have these tools, you can use the car's sun visors, the floorboard that covers the spare tire, a wheel cover, or the tire jack's base.

4. With the way cleared ahead of the drive wheels, wedge a floor mat under the treads and slowly drive free. Almost any roadside debris, rolled newspaper, magazines, twigs, or small tree limbs can also be used to build an escape ''road'' for snowed-in tires.

5. If your car has perforated wheels (designed with decorative holes), you can fashion crude but often effective ''rope chains'' by slipping a length of rope through the holes, drawing it over the tread, and securely tying it in place. Half a dozen segments of rope, tied over the drive treads, may provide enough traction to get you free.

6. Ice under the treads can complicate your best efforts, causing the wheels to spin. Spinning wheels produce heat. Heat can make ice slick. To free the wheels from slick ice, you may have no choice but to ''rock'' the car. To rock it, you successively and quickly shift the car from forward to reverse, building a back-and-forth

rhythm that inch-by-inch often overcomes the slickest ice. As you gain an inch, have a companion block the wheels with a rock or tree limb to prevent them from slipping back into the ice rut.

7. When driving out of a snow trap, you may have to shift into a low gear (Low in automatic transmissions, first gear for standard shifts) or power out in a higher, drive gear. Low gears give the most power, but precisely because of their power, they may needlessly spin the wheels and only dig them deeper. Higher gears deliver less power. Experts suggest first trying the less powerful drive gears (Drive for automatic transmissions, third gear or higher for standard transmissions).

8. Do not put extra weight (like rocks, sand, or sacks of cement) into the trunk or deflate the drive tires, thinking you can improve drive wheel traction that way. Front-wheel drive cars actually lose traction if you add weight in the trunk. The reason is obvious: weight in the rear tends to lift the drive wheels in front, reducing their snow grip. Despite this, some drivers with rear-wheel drive vehicles insist that weight in the trunk, over the rear wheels, improves traction.

As for deflating the drive tires, tire makers insist, and have tests to prove, that deflation actually puts less tread in contact with the snow, decreasing traction.

FREE A TIRE
FROZEN TO THE PAVEMENT

You leave the car out in cold weather, and in the morning when you start the engine and get into gear the car won't move either forward or in reverse. You're "iced."

More precisely, the tires have frozen to the pavement or in some rut or ground depression you didn't notice when you parked the car. "Icing" happens only when certain weather, road, or terrain conditions exist: wet snow or rain has to be falling, and water has to be around the tires just before a quick freeze.

Most tires frozen to the pavement can routinely be freed. Ice between the tread blocks (a tire's rubber tread design) will quickly break when you start the engine and slowly accelerate. But there are exceptions. For example, when the drive tires are deeply embedded in a mass of road or ground ice, sheer engine power won't work them loose. You've got to free them another way.

➤ WHAT TO DO

1. Try "rocking" the car to free it. In rocking, you shift into forward and then, while accelerating a little, reverse in a brief (seconds) but steady rhythm. Prolonged rocking can overheat transmissions, especially automatic transmissions.

   Don't accelerate more than 10 to 20 mph (despite what some owner's manuals say about briefly accelerating to speeds as high as 35 mph). If the tires suddenly break loose at a speed over 20 mph, you may lose control of your car.
2. If rocking doesn't work, you've got to attack the ice itself, either melting it or chipping it carefully away from the treads. (To get free, you usually only need to free the drive tires.)
3. For melting ice around tires, a gallon of hot—the hotter the better—water will usually melt enough to get you going. (Don't try to melt your way free if outside temperatures are well below freezing; otherwise, the hot water you slosh around the tires will also freeze.)

   In a dire emergency far from any spigot, and if your car's radiator has a petcock (a drain), you can use hot radiator antifreeze. (Although it melts ice better than water, you should only borrow a quart or two from your radiator, which generally holds from nine to 13 quarts of antifreeze.) Screw open the petcock at the bottom of the radiator, drain a quart of hot antifreeze into a container, then screw the petcock shut. The hot antifreeze should get your frozen tires free. At the next opportunity, replenish the antifreeze you borrowed.

4. Salt—even the grocery variety—will also melt ice around tires. But it works at a snail's pace. A quicker way to get free, if the temperature is too frigid for a hot water treatment, is simply to chip away the ice. Use a screwdriver, a hammer, a hatchet, an ice pick, or anything else that's handy to chip or pound with.

5. Depending on how much ice is holding your drive tires, you may have to work around all the treads, which may necessitate working partially under the car. Spread a blanket, the car floor mats, a tarp, or a coat as insulation against the cold pavement and ice.

6. Once you've melted or chipped away most of the ice gripping the drive treads, start the engine. Shift into the highest gear you can manage, if you have a standard transmission, or Drive for automatic transmissions. High gear delivers the least engine torque, reducing wheel spin. Accelerate slowly, and drive the wheels free.

YOUR BATTERY FREEZES

If your battery freezes, it tells you more about your car's electrical system and the battery's condition than about the weather. Ordinarily, a well-charged battery won't freeze. Even one with less than three-quarters charge can survive temperatures as low as −55°F.

If it freezes, you can be fairly sure of one of several things: your car's electrical system (the alternator or generator and voltage regulator), which normally keeps the battery up to proper charge, has failed to charge the battery; or the charge in the battery is extremely low—probably too low to start the car even if it were not frozen; or the battery will no longer accept a charge from the car's battery charging system or, in fact, from any other source.

A frozen battery is not something you can fix quickly. The problem isn't the weather; it's the battery or the car's charging system. Even if you thawed the battery, it is doubtful it would have enough power to start the car—unless it is recharged, assuming it can be. Once a battery freezes, its components can become damaged by the frozen electrolyte solution (which can expand and fracture the battery's case), or one of its essential cells can rupture. Once a battery has a dead cell, it is not amenable to a quick fix.

➤ WHAT TO DO

1. With a frozen battery you are faced with few choices. If you own a second car, you can borrow that car's battery. Or, you can ask a friend or neighbor to temporarily lend you a battery so you can drive to an automotive store and buy a new one. If you're on the highway, without the benefit of an auto club or other road service, you can get a ride to the next town or service station, buy a battery, return to your car, and install it.
2. Having replaced the battery, you should check your car's battery charging system to prevent another problem with a battery freezing or going dead.

SURVIVE A TWISTER OR TORNADO

If you have ever been in the path of a twister or tornado, or observed one from a distance, you already know they are deadly. They are earth's fiercest windstorms, and the open road is one of the worst places to be when they strike.

On average, more than 700 tornadoes strike across the United States each year. Although they can occur anywhere, in any state, and in any season, probably half of each year's tornadoes touch down in April, May, and June (December and January are virtually tornado free). Tornadoes occur most often in Texas, Oklahoma, Kansas, Nebraska, and Missouri. However, they strike almost as frequently in Arkansas, Alabama, and Mississippi. If there is a "tornado belt"—and statistics show that there is—it reaches from the Appalachian Mountains to the Rocky Mountains and through the Great Plains from the Gulf of Mexico into Canada.

A tornado's twin funnels chase fleeing motorists.

Although they can strike anywhere and at any time, tornadoes most often strike from midafternoon through early evening—and within a narrow time frame: 3 P.M. to 7 P.M., when thunderstorms (their source) are most apt to form.

Whereas scientists still have not wholly sorted out the gestation of tornadoes—from conception to birth—their toll of human life, property, and vehicles is only too well documented. During 16 hours one April, 149 tornadoes touched down in 13 states from Mississippi to Canada, killing 300, injuring 5,500, and costing millions of dollars in damage.

Tornadoes are unpredictable. Their destructive path can often be measured in yards or blocks, rather than in miles. They may touch down briefly, then retract into the thunderstorm to touch down again miles from their first hit. One of this century's most lethal tornadoes, moving at 62 mph (although the average ground speed for a tornado is more likely 30 to 40 mph), successively touched down a dozen times in its three-state, 219-mile course, leaving 689 people dead.

The average 200- to 300-mph winds within a tornado's characteristic funnel are strong enough to pick up and briefly carry heavily laden trucks, to say nothing of cars. These winds are far stronger than virtually any recorded hurricane winds. (In Nebraska, a truck loaded with 45 tons of sugar was lifted nearly 50 feet into the air and deposited atop a building.)

A "twister," a name mistakenly used synonymously with a tornado, is a wind of a different breed. Twisters are the familiar "dust devils" of circular winds that move across fields and highways. They are born not in thunderstorms but rather on the ground, or not far aboveground. Air temperature variations and other factors start the twister rotating and moving. Twisters are strictly local (they may roam across a single field or narrowly across a small stretch of highway), short-lived, and of limited danger to drivers and their cars.

Can you survive a tornado or keep control of your car if rocked by a twister?

➤ WHAT TO DO

If you see a twister moving toward you:

1. Quickly note its course. Twisters move in an often easily discernible path.
2. If a twister's path is almost certain to cross the highway ahead, slow or stop. Let it pass.
3. If you can't stop or elude a twister, slow down, hold the wheel tightly to keep control, keep your eyes on the road ahead (dust lifted by a twister can briefly obscure traffic), and ride it out. Twisters may briefly rock the car, making steering skittish or difficult, but seldom have the power to do more.

To minimize the chance of a tornado encounter:

1. If you have to drive through a tornado-prone area, and have a choice of when to travel, avoid driving during April, May, and June—the months of greatest tornado

frequency. During these months, and other tornado-prone months like July and August, be off the road by early afternoon. Avoid traveling between 3 P.M. and 7 P.M., when tornadoes most frequently threaten.

2. Don't drive at night. At night it is difficult to distinguish a brooding thunderstorm— the birthplace of tornadoes—from atmospheric disturbances of lesser threat. Nor can you spot a forming or fast-moving tornado funnel.

3. Listen to the radio. Don't set out for the road if local radio broadcasters announce a tornado watch (the preliminary alert given before a full-fledged tornado warning). A "watch" means that atmospheric conditions are right for the birth of a tornado. A "warning" is an alert to immediately seek shelter or invoke other defensive measures because a tornado has been spotted and is expected to touch down.

If you spot a tornado while driving:

1. A tornado should never catch you by surprise. If you are driving in a tornado area in "tornado season," tune your radio to a local station.

2. With or without forewarning, be alert to developing weather conditions. Brooding storm clouds should trigger a personal alert. If you see an ominous black cloud, a funnel—like a pointing finger—jabbing toward ground, this is a tornado.

When a tornado heads toward you while you are driving in town:

1. Find shelter immediately.

2. There is no safe place aboveground and no guaranteed safe place belowground. Abandon your car and seek shelter in a public building, a hotel, an office building— sturdy structures that have basements.

3. Once in the basement, seek a confined place—a closet, a small bathroom, a service pantry. Avoid large, expansive areas—such as large conference or meeting rooms— because their broad ceilings could collapse under the tornado's force.

   If you have a choice, pick a confined, windowless, belowground shelter in the northeast area of a building. Tornadoes most often strike from the south or west.

When a tornado heads toward you while you are driving on the highway:

1. If there are no buildings within quick and easy reach of your car (places with a likely basement), get out of the open.

   Quickly scan the road for possible highway culverts (the large drainage pipes that run beneath highways), road shoulder ditches (the deeper the better), or any place below ground level that offers some protection.

2. If you can't find shelter, abandon your car. It is likely the unsafest place on the road. Lie facedown in an open space, a ditch or even a dry creek bed, and cover your head with your hands to protect against wind-blown debris.

Should you attempt to elude a tornado?

1. The experts are unanimous: you can't outdrive or outrun an oncoming tornado's ground-sweeping funnel. Even if you turned around and headed in the opposite direction, it would almost certainly overtake you. Despite average speeds of 30 to 40 mph, some tornadoes have been clocked at twice that speed—and more.
2. Those drivers who have *eluded* tornadoes, have turned onto roads running at right angles to the menace, speeding away east or west from a funnel distantly approaching from the north or south. Almost always the eluders are familiar with local roads and with the actions of tornadoes in their local areas. If you aren't as knowledgeable, think twice before attempting to elude a tornado.

ESCAPE A HAILSTORM

If caught in a hailstorm, you've got to make a quick and calculated decision: is what's coming down merely a staccato of harmless ice pellets or something worse?

Some hailstones—from golf-ball to baseball size, and sometimes even larger—can impact your car at more than 100 mph. This can dent and dimple a car's sheet metal or plastic, even shatter a windshield or wipe out a convertible top. Repair costs can be considerable.

Hailstorms capable of damaging a car are relatively rare. That's what makes a bad storm a driving emergency. Most drivers don't expect them. (They usually strike during spring and summer—the thunderstorm season.) Scientists conclude that virtually every thunderstorm—9 out of 10—produces some hail. Most of it melts and turns into rain before reaching the ground.

Hailstone bombardments, also known as "summer shrapnel," annually do multimillion-dollar damage to farm crops and can devastate your car if the hailstones are large enough. The largest hailstone ever recorded in the United States measured 17½ inches around and weighed nearly two pounds. Hailstones can also travel at great speeds (the highest recorded speed is 200 mph).

In summer, you can expect to encounter hailstorms almost anywhere. Certain areas, however, are particularly noted for the frequency and ferocity of their hailstorms. One of them is "Hail Alley," some 600 square miles covering parts of Colorado, Wyoming, Kansas, and Nebraska.

➤ WHAT TO DO

If caught in town in a hailstorm:

1. If the bombardment is heavy and the hailstones large enough, you have only seconds to get your car under cover without incurring damage.
2. Head immediately for shelter—for example, a vacant carport, a pay garage, the protective canopy of a service station, or even beneath a large tree. In the heaviest, most potentially damaging of hailstorms, you may have less than 10 seconds to find protection for your car before costly damage is done.

If caught on the road in a hailstorm:

1. Find shelter for your car immediately. On rural roads and highways, roadside trees—if large and foliaged enough—may provide shelter.
2. Driving on a highway, pull to the shoulder beneath an overpass or bridge. Or, if near an off-ramp, exit to find shelter beneath trees or building overhangs or an underpass, usually near the exit where a local road or highway passes beneath the expressway.

SURVIVE A FLASH FLOOD

A flash flood, true to its name, is a flood that occurs in a flash. The cause is usually a cloudburst—a predictable, but maverick, rainstorm—that suddenly fills low-lying creeks, rivers, canyons, road dips, and culverts. Minutes or hours before, the terrain is dry. Then water from sudden local rains or, more frequently, from an unseen downpour far upstream rampages where before there was little or no water—and no apparent danger.

A flash flood's herculean torrents are capable of carrying heavy cars, campers, and trucks to their destruction. They seemingly appear from nowhere and cascade across roads, sweep over low-slung bridges, thunder down canyons, and inundate every low-lying path, including streets, rural roads, county roads, and older highways (those roads not engineered to prevent flash flooding).

Annually, flash floods—scarcely known to most drivers—kill more Americans than any other natural hazard, including hurricanes and tornadoes. According to statistics compiled by Richard Addison Wood, a former head of the National Weather Service's Disaster Preparedness and Awareness Program, more than half of the approximately 160 annual flash-flood fatalities are drivers, most of them swept to their deaths in cars while attempting to cross a flooded road dip, a wash, or a low-bridged stream or culvert.

No state or region is immune to flash-flood casualties. And whereas the Plains States and those across the desert West are most prone to flash flooding, Wood's survey of flash-flood deaths between 1945 and 1987 put Kentucky at the top of the fatalities list, followed closely by Texas, Mississippi, West Virginia, Missouri, Ohio, and Illinois.

➤ WHAT TO DO

Before setting out:

1. If you plan to drive on an unfamiliar road, listen to a road-and-weather report first. Local radio stations usually broadcast flash-flood alerts supplied by the National Weather Service.
2. Don't drive at night on unfamiliar roads during a flash-flood alert. Even if there is no alert, confine your driving to the daytime if the region you plan to drive through is

prone to flash floods. In daylight, you can often see the danger before you are upon it; at night, you seldom can.

If you drive at night in a region of frequent flash floods, or after a flash flood alert:

1. Drive at reduced speed so as not to outrun your headlights. You need to be able to see the road—as well as possible flood-prone washes, road dips, culverts, ravines, and canyons ahead.
2. Keep the radio tuned to local weather reports. If you hear a flash-flood alert, be especially cautious. If you observe threatening clouds or lightning anywhere around you—even at a great distance—double your caution. Distant rainstorms are the sources of many flash floods.

While driving anytime on flood-prone roads:

1. If you observe water flowing or even beginning to puddle across your way, stop immediately.
2. Do not attempt to cross any flooded stretch of road. What may appear to be a crossing you can ford, may conceal dips, mud holes, or washouts with water several feet deep. (A car can be carried away in less than two feet of water.)
3. Wait for the flood to recede. Many flash floods are short-lived. Even so, risk no crossing of a recently flooded stretch until you have gotten out of the car and carefully studied the roadway. There have been cases where impatient drivers, believing the way clear, have attempted to cross roads only to be mired in mud—and, moments later, hit by a second flash flood.

If caught in a flash flood:

1. If you are driving too fast to stop short of the flood or too close for effective braking, in the split second before you hit the water, try to steer upstream rather than letting the car get hit broadside and rolled over.
2. If your car is carried downstream, stay inside. It is safer than trying to jump from the car.

HOW TO

WEATHER TORRENTIAL RAIN

Being caught in a short-duration cloudburst, the lengthy deluge of a hurricane front, or something in between, torrential rain, even without accompanying wind, can test your emergency driving skills and concentration.

➤ WHAT TO DO

1. Switch on the windshield wipers to their fastest speed (and the rear window wipers, too, if your car has them).
2. Set your headlights on low beam. (Unlike high beams, low beams illuminate the road just ahead and prevent glare distracting to you and to oncoming drivers.) With lights turned on, your taillights are also on, warning drivers behind of your presence.
3. Turn on the windshield defrosters to prevent condensation (which can cloud your already decreased vision) from fogging the windshield.
4. Gird yourself against skidding. The downpour, plus residual oil and rubber residue, may combine to make the roadway especially slippery and your car especially skid prone.
5. Test your brakes. Apply them lightly and frequently to be sure they're working. In torrential downpours, brakes can become wet and malfunction even though you have not driven through standing water. Sometimes a wall of water from passing vehicles, especially trucks, can also wet brakes.

   To dry them out, use one foot to "work" the brakes with short applications, keeping your other foot on the accelerator to maintain your speed. (This is an old brake-drying trick. It's often used in emergencies when you need to dry the brakes but don't want to slow down or stop—as you might if you took your foot off the gas.) Slowing suddenly in a deluge may cause your car to be rear-ended. A few quick, light brakings usually produce enough friction heat to dry brake linings, restoring all or much of their efficiency without causing skidding.

If you decide to leave the highway or freeway:

1. Know where you're heading and where the nearest shelter is—for example, a service station, restaurant, highway rest area, or any place likely to provide shelter on

ground high enough to be reached without having to drive through puddles or raging water runoff.

Weigh your decision to leave the highway against anticipated off-road conditions. Secondary and rural roads usually flood easier in torrential downpours than do highways, which are engineered to withstand most flooding. In windstorms, there's the added danger of wind-blown debris, fallen electric lines, and downed trees.

2. Make no move to turn off the highway until you've signaled your intentions with sufficient "lead time"—as long as a minute in a blinding downpour—using your turn signal. Short, quick brake applications add a brake-light warning.
3. Once you've left the highway, drive slowly and find shelter.

If you opt to stop and park:

1. Sometimes it's wiser simply to pick a safe roadside stopping place and wait out the downpour. There may be a rest area just ahead, or a shoulder under a bridge or overpass, that can provide shelter out of the rain.
2. If none of these are available, the road's unprotected shoulder may be a safe waiting place, but only if it's wide enough for parking well off the highway, is free of running water, and is *paved*. Rule out unpaved shoulders. They may become mud or sand traps.
3. If you pull onto the shoulder, do so cautiously but decisively, after checking oncoming traffic in your rearview mirror. In a downpour, never give false road signals. Once you've signaled your intention to pull off the road and are sure the road is clear behind, make your move. Quickly get off the road and onto the shoulder.
4. When you are off the road, keep your headlights on. Or, if there is no immediate slacking of the downpour and you don't want to risk running down the battery, turn on the car's hazard or parking lights, or both. They consume far less energy than your headlights. Either way, make certain that other drivers are aware that you are parked on the shoulder.

If you decide to keep driving:

1. With your low-beam headlights on and your wipers going at their fastest speed, *concentrate* on driving through the deluge. If the car's radio or stereo is on, turn it off. Such distractions disturb your driving concentration.
2. Reduce speed to about 15 to 20 mph.
3. When traffic allows, move to the highway's "uphill" lane—usually the left lane or the one next to the centerline stripe or highway divider. All highways are designed with a "pitch" or a slope. The highest lane is usually the left lane. The built-in slope directs rainwater to the lowest lane, at the highway's shoulder. Lower-lying

shoulder lanes become flooded in torrential rain. It's easy to lose control—and suffer brake failure—if your wheels plow through water.

Another advantage of driving in the higher lane is that you can often see—and steer by—the centerline striping should rain reduce road visibility. If driving in the higher lane has a disadvantage, it's being splashed by cars traveling in the opposite direction.

4. Once you are in the left lane, stay there even if drivers high-beam you to move out of the way. Despite the downpour, some drivers insist on driving at unsafe speeds. In a blinding rain, you should not change lanes except to leave the highway. If cars want to pass you, let them change lanes to do so.

5. Drive alert to *hydroplaning*, the condition in which tire treads lose almost all traction with the road, converting your car into a kind of boat that literally planes over the road's surface. If your car begins to hydroplane, braking will have little or no effect. Even if your tires are in good condition (but especially if your tire treads are worn), rain, oil, and rubber can combine to slick the road's surface. Nothing but drastically reduced speed can prevent out-of-control hydroplaning.

Most drivers can safely drive through torrential rain if they reduce speed, apply their brakes frequently (but judiciously to wring them out), and concentrate—as calmly and as relaxed as possible—on traffic.

YOU CAN'T SEE
THROUGH THE WINDSHIELD

It's one thing to drive through a blinding snowstorm or downpour when you expect rain or snow to reduce your road vision. It's quite another when your vision is unexpectedly wiped out by mud, water, snow, or a newspaper across the windshield, obliterating road vision. The vision blackout may span only seconds, yet those few seconds can be critical on fast-trafficked, congested roads or streets.

You've got to act fast and keep control of the car, perhaps activating the washer fluid and turning on the wipers, but rein in the impulse to act rashly, to do something that might make matters worse, like braking in panic. If you panic, you may not remember where cars were just an instant before or the layout of the road.

Imagery is important whenever you take your eyes from the road—perhaps to tune in a different radio station, to shuffle papers on the seat beside you, or to adjust the rearview mirror. Even though you have momentarily taken your eyes from the road, you feel no trepidation or panic because you are confident you have mentally "positioned" traffic.

➤ WHAT TO DO

1. Don't panic.
2. Drive at the same speed, in the same traffic position. Do not brake. Do not swerve because your vision is obscured.
3. If snow, rain, or mud blocks out the windshield, quickly activate the windshield washer and wipers.
4. As you do, find a spot to look through. Until you manage to clear the windshield, it will have to provide enough road vision for driving.
5. As the windshield clears, confirm and maintain your road position.

THE BRAKES BECOME WET AND FAIL

It may have happened to you. You drive through a flooded intersection or perhaps only an axle-high puddle. Moments later when you brake, nothing happens. The car hardly slows. The pedal feels normal, but you have no brakes. The brake linings are wet. In a moment of panic, you realize you can't stop.

➤ WHAT TO DO

1. Take your foot off the gas.
2. Quickly downshift to a lower, engine-braking gear.
3. "Pump" the brakes. Because there's plenty of brake fluid, pumping the pedal will apply the brakes even if they're wet and unresponsive. Pump them gently at first, then harder (this generally restores them faster than hard braking from the start).

   Since the mechanical scraping of the rotor by the pads produces friction, pumping the brakes should produce enough heat to quickly dry the brake linings. Once dried, their stopping ability will be restored.
4. If you're careful not to drive through any more standing water while you pump them, your brakes should return to normal and stop the car well short of any traffic ahead. Usually the car's brakes can be dried, and fully restored, by braking on and off about a dozen times.

HOW TO

PROTECT YOURSELF IN A SANDSTORM

Highway sandstorms are not to be confused with dust storms or with their seasonal (usually July and August) Arizona cousins, "haboobs." Both may blot out the view ahead, often bringing traffic to a precarious standstill, and both may be accompanied by fierce winds.

That, however, is where the similarity ends. Sandstorms are sometimes powered by 60 to 100 mph winds. In a matter of minutes (or seconds), tiny grains of abrasive sand can sandblast a car's expensive finish right down to bare metal or raw plastic.

The sand may also cause engine damage—often unsuspected by motorists who have successfully driven through a sandblast. Sand can infiltrate the engine compartment and the interior of the car. Oil and air filters can become gritted with sand, and in the worst storms, so can the fuel tank and the gasoline. Car lubricants—engine oil, transmission fluid, and power-steering fluid—can be coated with sand and ruin the engine, automatic transmission, and power-steering mechanism.

Sandstorms usually strike where highway sand dunes—as contrasted to the firmer desert soil—are exposed to the wind. As wind velocity increases, the wind skims the tops of the dunes, sandblasting everything in its path.

Some Western states post signs on the desert roads and highways, like "Blowing Sand, Reduce Speed," to warn motorists of frequent sandstorm areas. In sandblast corridors, there may be no evidence of wind or even sand. But don't be fooled. Sandblasts do habitually strike— true to posted warnings.

If caught in a sandstorm, you've got to make a quick decision: drive through it or seek immediate shelter.

Drivers familiar with the nature of sandstorms know some sandblast corridors are only a few hundred yards wide, while others stretch for miles. In a narrowly confined sandblast area, drivers can reduce speed (due to restricted visibility and to reduce sand impact) and drive through the storm, often without damage to their cars' paint jobs or engine parts.

Some sandstorms rage only for a few minutes, then abate. Others continue for hours, even days. For drivers unfamiliar with an area, judging the different kinds of sandstorms is difficult, if not impossible. Listening to local storm reports can help, unless you've already driven into a sandstorm.

34

➤ WHAT TO DO

1. Slow down, switch on the headlights (visibility may be only a few yards ahead), and come to a quick decision: drive through it, on the assumption you have entered a narrow sandblast corridor; turn back, in hopes of driving out of the sandstorm; or seek shelter.

    The raging sandstorm around you, in all probability, is extensive, perhaps miles ahead and behind you. You must assume that strong winds are blowing over much of the highway—and may continue for hours. You cannot drive through it without serious damage to your car. You must find shelter before the sandblast indelibly damages your car.

2. Finding shelter in so short a time on the open road may be impossible. But, with no other choice, you have to try. Head for any place out of the sandblast: a service station or garage, a building that will protect the car from the full force of wind-blown sand, or a highway embankment or overpass structure that will act as a shield.

3. Once you have found shelter, park facing into the wind, to minimize exposing the car to stray, swirling wind blasts. Unless you've found shelter behind a restaurant or some other place that is open for business, stay in the car with the windows and vents shut tight and the engine off.

4. In a sandstorm, be cautious when exiting the car. If you must, hold a handkerchief over your face and mouth. Wind-driven sand can sting your face and your body, even through a couple of layers of clothing. Sandstorms can also injure unprotected eyes and get into your lungs. People with respiratory problems may find breathing difficult in a storm.

5. Once the winds have abated, drive slowly to the nearest service station (unless you have found shelter in one). Have an attendant or mechanic open the hood and check for sand infiltration.

    Play it safe with your engine. Have the engine oil changed. Have new air and oil filters installed. Ask the mechanic to check the transmission and power-steering fluids for sand (although it is difficult for sand to infiltrate these systems because they are sealed). If sand is present, the mechanic should drain either or both and refill with fresh fluid. If sand has seriously invaded the engine compartment, have it flushed out with air, water, or steam, or remove the sand with a vacuum cleaner.

6. Not until the engine compartment is sand free—and the danger of engine or transmission damage eliminated or minimized—is it really safe to continue on your way.

YOU ARE CAUGHT IN AN EARTHQUAKE

Like most drivers, your first reaction is apt to be puzzlement, as the hills bordering the highway suddenly seem to erupt and spew clouds of dust. The road ahead suddenly undulates, as the concrete rises and falls. Your car shakes violently. You are caught in a major earthquake.

Earthquakes—unlike blizzards, tornadoes, thunderstorms, and other natural phenomena—give no visual warning. In fact, no warning at all.

Caught in a major earthquake on the highway, you may suddenly be wrestling with a force you can't see or even recognize. You know instinctively that something is wrong, that you face an emergency. But you don't know what is really wrong or what is causing the car to shake or to feel as if all four tires have gone flat. The quake may come and go before you recognize what it is.

In an earthquake, highway overpasses can collapse, whole sections of roadway can be uprooted, fissures can open ahead of you. Yet a car may be among the safest places to be when a major quake strikes.

➤ WHAT TO DO

When driving on the highway:

1. In the seconds that the earthquake rules the highway, think fast, act fast. Grip the wheel hard as it tries to tear itself out of your hands. Steer straight, whatever the effort. Keep control.
2. Do whatever you have to do to keep the car in your lane. Quake forces may cause your car to involuntarily switch lanes. Steer hard to maintain your lane position.
3. Take your foot off the gas pedal. Let the car slow down. As you do, quickly observe traffic around you, particularly ahead, in your lane and in the oncoming lane or lanes.
4. Head for—or remain in—the open. The open road (not an overpass or any structure spanning the highway) is your best shelter. As is your car.
5. If you're on an overpass, in a highway tunnel, on a bridge, or approaching any struc-

ture over the highway, speed up or slow down to avoid passing beneath or through any structure during a quake.

6. Be alert to the possibility of a fissure opening ahead of you. Quake fissures are generally narrow (a few inches to a few feet wide) and shallow. But running into or crossing one can flatten tires, throw the car out of control, or do major front-end and other damage. Despite what you've seen in the movies, fissures won't swallow your car. Most, in fact, never cross a highway. When they do they are usually quickly filled in by the collapsing roadbed.

7. As soon as the quake is over, pull to the shoulder and stop. Tune the radio to a local station. Listen for road advisories. If overpasses or bridges ahead are down or damaged, find a route around them (if you need help, ask other drivers or call the police).

When driving in town:

1. Stay in the lane you're driving in, slow down, and quickly observe what's happening around you.

2. Whatever is happening, do two things fast: get into the lane farthest from the curb, or into the center of the street (to avoid being hit by objects falling from buildings), and get into the open. If you find an open place—with no buildings, wires, overhangs, or tall trees nearby—stop there, unless you're obstructing traffic.

3. When the quake is over, heed your radio's local advisories. Proceed cautiously. There could be any number of obstructions ahead, from fallen debris to broken water or gas mains. Be especially vigilant for downed power lines. Do not drive over them. Your car is not an insulator against high voltage.

4. If you must park, don't venture into a closed structure, such as a parking garage. Aftershocks can be almost as strong as the initial quake. Buildings and other structures that survived the first shock may not survive those following. Park in the open on the street (or better, in a large mall or supermarket parking lot).

5. If you get out of the car, continue your vigilance. Aftershocks can cause already loosened or weakened structures to collapse. Until aftershocks appear to be over, do not walk near tall buildings. Even if they appear structurally sound, glass from shattered windows can be dangerous.

HOW TO

BEAT THE ODDS OF BEING STRUCK BY LIGHTNING

Getting caught in a lightning storm is a possible life-or-death situation. Statistically, however, few cars or their drivers are struck by lightning. Most frequently hit are golfers (especially those who seek shelter under trees), outdoor workers, and recreationists, particularly boaters and swimmers.

In a lightning storm, there is no telling where or when lightning will strike. But from years of research, one thing seems clear: your car is a relatively safe place to be in a violent lightning storm, provided you work fast to maximize its potential protection.

In a severe lightning storm, park away from water, bridges, pipelines, railroad tracks, power lines, and tall trees.

➤ WHAT TO DO

1. Stay in the car. Roll up the windows. If you are in a convertible, close the top. Retract your radio antenna.
2. Avoid making your car a target. If you pull off the road, don't park beneath a tall tree, near water (whether a pond, river, or lake), close to metal fencing, railroad tracks, high-tension power lines, wires, aboveground piping, radio or communications towers, or metal-roofed farm or ranch buildings. Don't park near or drive over metal bridges.
3. While driving or parked, avoid being an isolated target or a target generally higher than surrounding terrain. If you are driving uphill in an area devoid of trees or other tall structures, your car may inadvertently become an isolated, high target. If you feel you are in danger of being struck, drive to a lower elevation where there are taller structures.
4. If you are driving in a forest and can't escape being near or beneath trees, avoid areas of extremely tall trees. Pull off the road and park near smaller trees. When a forest is struck by lightning—which happens frequently—the tallest trees are most often hit.

HOW TO

BEAT BLINDING SUNLIGHT

"**S**un" highways—most of them beelining east and west—too often subject drivers to blinding, late afternoon sun. In heavy traffic, you may find yourself straining to see. Under these conditions, the sun is a blazing torch, making your eyes smart and obliterating traffic ahead.

➤ WHAT TO DO

1. Slow down. In all likelihood, traffic around you has slowed down, too. Other drivers may also be blinded by the sun.

A piece of cardboard supplements sun visors to thwart the blinding sun.

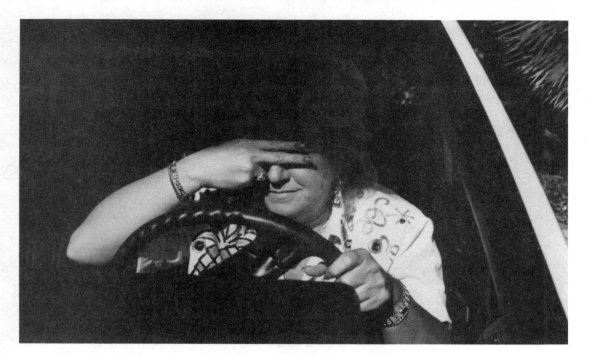

To beat the blinding sunlight, use a two-finger "sun mask."

2. Make a quick decision: should you stay on the road or exit? If you exit, you can take a less-trafficked side road or street where buildings and other structures may wholly or partially block the sun's blinding rays. Or you might decide to stop for a cup of coffee and wait out the sun's setting.

   In most situations, the sun will shortly dip low enough so that driving is less dangerous. Usually you need wait only 10 to 30 minutes before returning to the highway.

3. If you stay on the road, pull the sun visors down, put on sunglasses, and squint. Squinting, when you're driving directly into the sun, is often more effective than sunglasses. As for the sun visors, they may be ineffective. Visors are designed to shut out the sun's rays when the sun is relatively high in the sky. When the sun is low, its blinding glare eludes the visors.

4. If, while squinting, you're still blinded by the sun, try looking through a "finger mask." Hold the index and middle fingers of one hand apart a little. Steer with the other hand. Hold your finger mask over one eye (one eye is enough to safely drive by, provided it has good vision), and peer through the aperture created by your slightly spread fingers.

   A finger mask shuts out all but a narrow sliver of sun glare. You can reduce the glare even more—and still see the highway and its traffic—by narrowing the space between your fingers.

While less effective than a finger mask, holding up a magazine or piece of cardboard may shut out most of the sun's blinding glare.

5. If your commute is frequently plagued by blinding sun, consider a more permanent cure for the glare. Fix an extension to your car's visors to extend their reach. Tape a piece of cardboard or a heavily tinted piece of stout plastic to the width of the visors, long enough to shut out most of the sun's glare while still maintaining road visibility.

HOW TO

FREE A SAND-TRAPPED CAR

The worst sand traps are not on a golf course. They lie in wait, little suspected by most drivers, along thousands of miles of highways and rural roads, beyond roadways, as well as along lake shores and at creekside camping and picnicking places. Sand traps are a part of nature—and of driving.

Pull off the highway to check your car, or merely for a roadside picnic, and one wheel or another may sink into sand or another unstable material. Decide to turn around on a rural road where there is no good place to turn around, and you may back into trouble: sand up to your axles. Move off the road surfaces most of us drive on—concrete, asphalt, or gravel—and you may be sand-trapped.

➤ WHAT TO DO

1. Turn off the ignition. When wheels spin, they only dig themselves deeper. Spinning your wheels can also overheat and damage an automatic transmission. It is equally useless, although not as immediately damaging, in the case of a manual transmission. Either way, you're stuck. No amount of power to the drive wheels is going to free you. Your wheels need traction.

2. The quickest way to get traction is to lay something just ahead and under the forward edge of the mired treads, in the direction you want to drive free. The material should be something tire treads can get a grip on: the car's floor mats, the trunk's floor liner, a sturdy towel, a bulky article of clothing (like a coat), or tire chains.

3. With the material laid ahead of the mired wheels, put the transmission in low gear— its pulling gear—and very gently accelerate. The aim is to get the wheels to grip and pull themselves free.

4. If that doesn't free the wheels, try digging. Beneath the loose sand trapping your wheels you may find hard-packed sand. It can almost be as hard as a road surface. Get down to the hard-packed sand and your wheels will have enough traction to get the car moving.

    To reach this hard surface, you will need something to dig with. If you don't have a shovel, use the base plate of a car jack, a metal wheel cover, a camper's sauce pan, a license plate, or even a coffee can.

43

The mat is placed under the tread in the direction you want to drive.

Usually, it's not enough to remove the loose sand around and immediately in front of the stuck treads. You may have to scoop out a wheel path several feet or yards ahead of the treads to prevent their getting stuck again.

5. As a last resort, use another vehicle with a winch or towline to pull your car free, but be sure the line (rope or steel) is hooked or tied to your car's frame, not to the bumper. Bumpers seldom have the strength to withstand pulling.

6. As the stuck wheels begin to find traction and roll, chock them (or chock the steered wheels) to prevent the car from rolling back into the sand trap. To chock them (see How to Block Wheels to Prevent Roll-Away, page 109), wedge a piece of wood or a large rock behind the steered or drive wheels as the mired wheels come unstuck. As the stuck wheels find traction and inch out of the trap, keep moving the chocks so the tires can't slip back.

HOW TO

GET UNSTUCK FROM MUD

You're mired in mud. Applying even a little power to the wheels only spins them deeper in the goo. But there are ways you can get unstuck.

In fact, the same methods used for freeing a car from a sand trap (see How to Free a Sand-Trapped Car, page 43) can also be applied to a car stuck in mud. But mud—because it is slipperier than sand (or even snow) and because it is wetter—can prevent stuck wheels from getting traction where they might if stuck in sand.

➤ WHAT TO DO

1. In mud, the "displacement method" often gets wheels unstuck quickly. What you do is displace the mud and water with something more stable—rocks, sand, gravel, tree limbs. Thrown into the mud hole, these objects move the water away from the wheels and provide the traction needed to free the car. If possible, use a piece of wood to firmly pack the objects you've placed around the wheels. Packing firms and solidifies the displacement material.

FREE A CAR FROM
A ROAD RIDGE OR ROCK

The surprisingly fragile underbellies of many of today's cars are not meant for rock climbing. Neither were most (with the exception of off-road vehicles) designed for scaling ridges. That's why getting free may be difficult if your car gets hung up on a high road ridge or somehow ends up on a rock. Another problem may be freeing the car without rupturing its oil pan, disturbing the transmission, destroying the muffler and tailpipe, or doing other undercarriage damage.

How, then, do you free your car from a road ridge or rock with minimum damage to the car?

➤ WHAT TO DO

1. Carefully size up your predicament. This means getting a full view under your car. You may have to lie on your back or stomach to do it, or wriggle beneath the chassis. Make absolutely certain that the ridge is supporting the car, and that it is safe to get beneath it.

2. Note what parts are likely to be damaged if you attempt to drive off the obstruction. Also note the direction you should drive, if your wheels have enough traction, to do the least damage. If the car is hung up *ahead* of the oil pan (the usually flat, squarish reservoir just behind the engine), plan to back off the obstacle, rather than going forward. Backing off will avoid oil pan damage. If you have a choice of sparing the oil pan by backing up on the muffler and tailpipe, do it. They aren't essential to a car's driveability.

3. Having decided either to back up or move forward, shift to the appropriate gear: reverse to back off, lowest drive gear to go forward. Very slowly, inch the car off the obstruction. Keep inching even if you hear metal scraping and even if something is being torn loose (you've already sized up which parts may be damaged).

4. If you can't inch off, and lack a winch (the standard device for pulling a car off an obstruction), try any of several other methods.
    One tactic is to push the car off the high point with another car. Before attempt-

ing this, again carefully observe where and how the car is lodged. You may note that the car is hung up on only one car part. If you can push the car off the point of obstruction, you may be able to back or drive free, even though the action may still do some damage.

Another way to free yourself is to jack up the car (from the side, front, or rear) and push it off the jack. When the car is pushed off the jack, it will move a few inches. That may be enough to dislodge the car.

When jacking the car up, be careful to stay well clear of the jack, and push the car while standing to the side, or from the front or rear (depending on which way it is likely to roll). You may have to jack and push several times before you can drive free.

5. If none of these methods work, you have little choice but to summon a tow truck or flag down a passing driver to get help. A vehicle with a winch can quickly pull your car free, although not necessarily without some damage.

PART 2

SITUATIONAL EMERGENCIES

OBJECTS ARE THROWN FROM AN OVERPASS

Approaching an expressway's overpass, you're suddenly aware that someone up on top is throwing objects at passing cars. Unfortunately, these incidents are not uncommon. Sometimes they involve malicious youngsters who may throw harmless objects; at other times they involve people who throw bricks or beer bottles. These projectiles may crash through a windshield, seriously injuring or killing someone driving by.

In the daytime, you may have enough time to evade a thrower; at night, you may not even be aware a thrower is on an overpass ahead.

In daytime, you can often avoid driving within a thrower's range; at night, you may not be aware there is a thrower on the overpass.

➤ WHAT TO DO

If you spot a daytime thrower:

1. Slow down, signal your intent to change lanes, brake fast if the way is clear, and get immediately to the shoulder.
2. Be especially cautious of "scrambling" traffic. When other drivers become aware of an overpass thrower—or when a car has been hit, perhaps causing it to swerve or even to crash—cars may scramble or scatter on the road ahead of you.
3. Whatever the risks, avoid driving within throwing range or beneath the overpass. Actually, your chance of being struck by random throwing is small. But if you are hit, the object (bricks and bottles are among the most dangerous) can crash through the windshield. You cannot gamble on the thrower's bad aim. (Actually, throwers seldom "aim." Rather, they calculate the speed of an oncoming car and time an object's drop.)
4. From the shoulder, observe the thrower's movements. Most throwers don't linger long. Having hit a car, or scrambled oncoming traffic, they may flee in fear of the police.
5. Do not proceed under the overpass until it is safe.
6. Immediately call 911 and alert police, either from your car phone or from the nearest public phone.

If you spot a thrower at night:

1. If you spot a thrower at night, it may be too late to avoid driving beneath the overpass. But darkness increases the odds that you won't get hit.
2. If scrambling traffic suggests trouble ahead, do as you would in daylight. Get to the shoulder and stop.
3. If you are unable to stop, try to divert the thrower. Sound your horn as you approach the overpass. Don't, however, high-beam your headlights. This may rivet his or her attention on your car. A horn blasting may be enough to stay the thrower's hand and cause him or her to flee.
4. Moments before you pass beneath the thrower's position, temporarily switch off your headlights. In darkness, this will black out your car until you are safely past the danger.
5. As in daylight, alert police as soon as you can.

GET MOVING AFTER A FENDER BENDER

After a minor traffic accident, most drivers exchange information (driver's license and plate numbers, names, addresses, phone numbers, and insurance data). The police may also be notified to make out a report. Annually, 20 million drivers (one driver in every seven) are involved in automobile accidents, the vast majority of them fender benders.

But before you drive away from a seemingly minor accident, you should consider whether your car is safe to drive.

➤ WHAT TO DO

1. Walk around the car, giving it a quick but close inspection.
2. Before making a decision to have it towed or driving it away from the scene of the accident, start the engine, work through the gears, and, unless a fender or another car part is obstructing the wheels, drive it forward and backward a few feet. As with most cars involved in fender benders, it will almost certainly pass a basic mechanical checkup.
3. Make any minor adjustments you can to make the car driveable. For example, if the fender is pushed up against a tire, see if you can pull the fender—while protecting your hands with a rag—away from the tire until it no longer makes contact. If you have a flat tire, put on the spare. If one end of a bumper is sagging, use rope or wire to secure it so that it doesn't drag on the pavement. Also tie down the hood, the trunk, or any doors that are ajar. Bandage any cracked glass with tape. If a wheel is bent, see if it wobbles when driven (this will almost certainly make steering difficult). A wheel with a minor wobble, common in fender benders, can usually be safely driven a short distance to a repair shop.

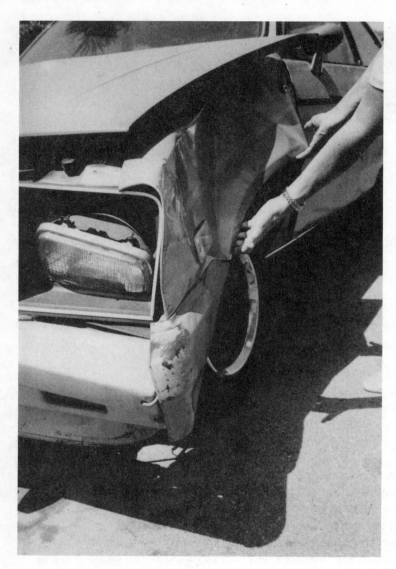

To get moving after a fender-bender, you must often bend the fender more to prevent it from scraping the tire.

AVOID A DRUNK DRIVER

From nearly half a mile's distance you suspect it. From a quarter mile, as the oncoming car draws ever closer, you are sure of it. The driver of the fast-approaching vehicle is drunk.

Asleep at the wheel? That's a possibility, too. But as you observe the car, you grow more certain that its driver is drunk, not simply asleep. (A car with a dozing driver tends to drift rather than weave, straddles traffic lines, and fails to dim bright lights for oncoming drivers.)

The emergency decision facing you is unnerving—whether this is your first or tenth road encounter with a possible drunk driver—but you have to think and act as fast as possible. You've got to decide whether the approaching driver is drunk or asleep at the wheel.

If the oncomer is asleep, switching on your headlights and then quickly alternating between high and low beams, whether in darkness or daylight, may arouse the driver. He or she will probably regain control of the car in time to get back in the proper lane.

If the oncomer is drunk, however, you probably can't, nor do you want, to arouse him or her. (If it is a late weekend night, around bar-closing time, the chances are that you're dealing with a drunk.) Aroused, the person's driving might become even more erratic and unpredictable.

Either way, you want only to avoid the oncoming car: to slip past, on your side of the road or highway if possible, without a collision or even a close brush.

➤ WHAT TO DO

If a suspected drunk driver approaches you on a two- or four-lane highway:

1. Do nothing to disturb the driver. Do nothing to attract his or her attention to you or your car. Don't flick your headlights.
2. If you're in the lane closest to the approaching car, quickly get over to the farthest lane—the lane closest to the highway's shoulder. Or, on a two-lane highway, onto the shoulder itself.
3. Slow down, but don't stop. You may have to take quick evasive action.
4. The car will probably pass you without mishap. But if it heads for your lane and a collision seems imminent, take any evasive action you must to get out of the way. If

this means riding the highway's shoulder, or turning onto a side road, or even moving into the drunk driver's side of the road (if he or she has already moved into yours), do it.

5. As soon as the drunk driver has passed, drive to a place with a telephone and alert local police, the highway patrol, the nearest sheriff's office, or phone 911 to report that a dangerous driver, probably drunk, is on the highway (give the direction the car is headed in).

If a suspected drunk driver, whether in town or on the highway, is just ahead of you—in your lane or in an adjacent lane—going in your direction:

1. In fast traffic, slow down and keep well behind the car. When traffic permits, move to the lane farthest from the car. Don't follow the car, if you can help it.
2. Don't speed up to pass. Don't attempt to get around. Don't honk your horn. If at night, don't flash your headlights.
3. In slow traffic, keep well behind the car and bide your time. Many intoxicated drivers are slowpokes.
4. Stifle the urge to pass until you have carefully studied his or her driving. If the driver is merely a dawdler, and his or her driving not noticeably erratic, consider passing. If the way is clear, and there's plenty of space in your intended passing lane, speed up and quickly pass the car. Keep moving until you are well ahead.
5. At the first opportunity, alert police.

AVOID A WRONG-WAY DRIVER

In daylight or darkness, the wrong-way driver is a highway nemesis. Surviving a confrontation with a wrong-way driver tests your driving skills, alertness, and nerves. If you fail to respond correctly, a head-on collision may result in a fatal injury.

With a wrong-way driver, you cannot make the assumption that you are dealing with a drunk driver (see How to Avoid a Drunk Driver, page 55). You have to treat the wrong-way driver as a potential killer. The driver may even be suicidal. Perhaps suicidal *and* drunk. Even if he or she is only a confused driver with a misguided sense of direction, that individual is nonetheless capable of taking the lives of innocent motorists.

➤ WHAT TO DO

1. As cars ahead scramble out of the way, scramble with them. Don't wait. Often a wrong-way driver is upon you before you realize it.
2. Get to the shoulder, if you can. Get as far out of the driver's path, or what appears to be the path, as possible.
3. To avoid a possible head-on collision, take whatever action is necessary. This may mean violating road safety rules. For example, if getting out of the way means changing lanes without signaling cars behind or means swerving behind or ahead of cars on adjacent lanes, do it.
4. As you scramble, don't unnecessarily call attention to your car, don't flash your headlights, and don't sound your horn.
5. When you are safely past the driver, alert the police.

A wrong-way driver may ignore warnings like this one.

RELAX WHILE DRIVING

For some, road stress, especially on fast-moving, trafficked roads, can become an emergency. Road stress can diminish alertness, how you react to traffic, even the ability to steer clear of trouble.

A simple regimen of exercises you can do in the car, like the ones devised by Dr. Laurence E. Morehouse, former Director of the Human Performance Laboratory at the University of California at Los Angeles, can alleviate highway fatigue, sharpen road perception, and buoy driver judgment. When practicing these exercises, remember to maintain your driving vigilance.

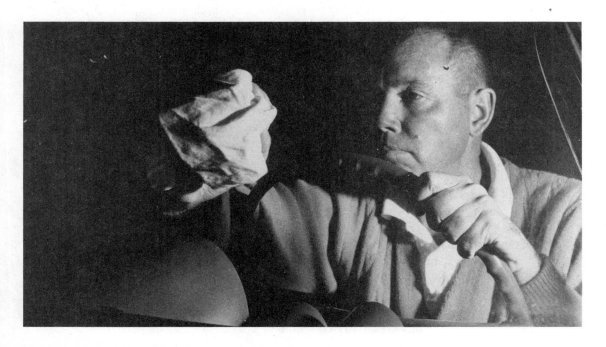

Engage in activity to relax while driving.

➤ WHAT TO DO

1. Wiggle your toes. Seat pressure blocks circulation, causing blood to mass in the feet and legs (the reason for the tingling sensation while driving). Reduced circulation means reduced blood, thus less oxygen goes to the brain, and drowsiness sets in.

    Wiggle your toes every 15 minutes or so to ''pump'' the leg muscles, restoring blood flow to the legs as well as to the brain.

2. Grasp and release the steering wheel. Clench the wheel hard, until knuckles whiten, then relax your grasp. Repeat at least 10 times. Hand and arm exercises ease tension.

3. Refocus your eyes. Simultaneous with toe wiggling and wheel grasping, practice a calculated eye exercise. Changing eye focus (if only to squint at a bug on the windshield) prevents visual fatigue. During long drives, spend 30 seconds out of every 15 minutes focusing and refocusing your eyes. You can make a quick eye exercise of gauge or dashboard watching.

4. Pivot your head. Move your head to the extreme right and left—as far as you can turn it without reducing road visibility. Doing so exercises muscles in back of the neck, pumping extra blood to the brain.

5. Breathe deeply. Breathe from the belly. Take a big breath and expel it. Breathe heavily and exhale half a dozen times every 15 minutes or so. Deep breathing increases oxygen intake and alertness.

6. Let your shoulders fall. As you breathe deeply, relax as much as you safely can. Let your shoulders fall. Let them feel heavy.

7. Let your weight sink deep into the seat. Slumping and redistributing your body weight exercises the upper body, increasing circulation.

8. Engage in some activity. It doesn't matter what you do, so long as you do something: reach for the glove compartment, raise or lower a sun visor, dust off the dash, stomp the floorboard with your free foot. Do anything that breaks the driving routine and exercises your hands and legs.

9. Talk to yourself. If you're driving alone, you can talk to yourself. You can also sing along with the radio.

10. Change your seat position. If you spend 15 minutes driving in one position, for example, with your back pressed into the seat, change that position, if only a few inches. Move forward to the seat's edge, then slump back into your original position. You'll feel relaxed. Tension—and much of the road anxiety—will waft away.

A simple driving regimen like this, repeated frequently, can help to maintain your alertness and reduce road stress whether on a daily commute or a cross-country drive.

GET HELP ON THE ROAD

$\mathbf{S}$tranded on a busy highway, many drivers become too timid to help themselves. "Stage fright overwhelms them," one expert says. From the anonymity of their cars, they are suddenly thrust onstage before a never-ending flow of cars.

If you need help on a highway, do whatever you must (within the confines of personal safety) to get it.

➤ WHAT TO DO

1. If you have a car phone and are an auto club member, help is only a push button away.

Signal your emergency with the universal motorist's distress signal: a raised hood.

61

2. Use the universal highway distress signals: raise your hood, tie something white or bright from an antenna or tucked into a door handle or window facing traffic, or use flares or emergency reflectors.

3. Many drivers will not stop for a motorist pulled to the shoulder (they may not want to become involved or may not have time to be). Nonetheless, waving your arms from the shoulder at oncoming cars often flags down a good samaritan when other attempts to get help fail.

4. Special circumstances to the contrary (for example, if you see an open convenience store just ahead or just off a nearby exit), stay with the car. The police, a highway maintenance crew, or a tow truck (omnipresent on many roads) will be along in time. Aside from the personal risks of leaving your car, you should stay with it (lock the doors and windows at night) simply to be able to respond to help when it arrives.

YOUR DRIVER LOSES CONSCIOUSNESS

Y̲ou're a passenger of a car traveling at highway speed when suddenly the driver loses consciousness, his or her hands still gripping the wheel. Perhaps it's a heart attack, a seizure, or a stroke. The reason isn't important, nor is your own traumatic shock. What's demanded now, as your unguided car heads at high speed toward almost certain disaster, is quick—and forceful—action.

The actions you take—must take—may span only seconds, but they may be the most important and momentous seconds in your life or in the life of your driver.

➤ WHAT TO DO

1. With your left hand, grasp the steering wheel. With your right, unfasten your seat belt. You can't do what you have to do restrained, your movements limited.
2. Shove the unconscious driver as far toward the driver-side door as possible, free yourself from your seat belt and shoulder harness, and shift your right hand onto the wheel.
3. With your *right* hand now on the steering wheel, muster all your strength and shove the unconscious body as far to the left and away from normal driving position as you can.
4. If the driver's hands still grasp the wheel, release them with a chop from your left hand—your free hand. (Chop with your fingers held tightly together and thrust *upward* against the unconscious driver's wrists.)
5. With the driver shoved out of driving position and his or her hands released from the wheel, take control of the car. If the driver's foot is still on the gas pedal, kick it free with your left foot. Or, if necessary, use your left hand (while still keeping an eye on the road) to push the foot off the accelerator.
6. Don't remove the key from the ignition. Don't turn off the ignition. Keep steering control of the car (with the gas pedal released) as it begins to slow.
7. If the car has an automatic transmission, get into second gear. Every down-gear—from Drive to Second to First—progressively slows the engine and car. Gradually, but often surprisingly quickly, as you down-gear, the engine will "brake" the car.

   If the car has a manual transmission and is in drive gear, leave the setting as is. You cannot downshift without using the clutch, which is probably unreachable

Steer with your left hand as you work to shove the driver out of the way.

from your position. And even if it were, in cars with between-seat standard shifts you are likely to be sitting on the gearshift and unable to reach it easily or properly downshift in time.

8. What about the brakes? From the passenger seat you are in no position to apply them unless you can somehow slip behind the wheel—either sitting on the lap of the driver or squeezed in beside him or her.

9. Switch on the car's four-way hazard lights to warn cars behind and ahead of a problem.

10. As you steer for the shoulder of the road, the car's speed slowed down to a crawl (assuming it has automatic transmission and you've downshifted into First—the car's most efficient self-braking gear), downshift once more to Neutral. With no power to the wheels, you should be able to bring the car to a stop on the shoulder, due in part to the ''braking friction'' generated by the tires and the pavement or shoulder. If you're lucky, you'll find an upgrade.

   For a manual transmission in neutral, it will take a bit longer for the car to slow down and stop.

11. Once stopped, switch off the ignition to kill the engine. For an automatic transmission, brake by putting the transmission in Park. If you have a manual transmission, attempt to shift into a gear. If you can't, apply the hand emergency brake.

SURVIVE A COLLISION
WITH A LARGE ANIMAL

In 1990, Michigan's licensed hunters killed 434,340 deer. In the same year, its licensed drivers killed 48,233. The National Highway Traffic Safety Administration estimates that each year 350,000 deer are killed by motorists. Pennsylvania authorities estimate that 1 in 20 of its deer population will die in a vehicle collision.

However, just as cars kill an uncounted number of wild and domestic animals, a collision with an animal can kill a driver (upon impact, an animal—especially a large deer or cow—can be hurled through a windshield). Annually, more than 100 drivers die and 8,000 are injured in animal collisons. Sometimes injury results when a driver swerves off the road to avoid hitting an animal. Applying brakes on an icy road can send a car into a lethal skid.

Animal collisions are among the most harrowing, grisly, and avoidable (in many cases) of all driving emergencies. Drivers are at fault more often than animals. Drivers often ignore animal crossing or habitat area signs because they don't see any animals. (Many animals are nocturnal; come darkness or dawn, they often appear exactly where the signs are posted.)

Thousands of miles of highway are posted with OPEN RANGE signs, meaning the highway runs through an unfenced area where domestic animals have as much right to graze along a highway as a motorist has to drive it.

Few drivers realize that their headlights—especially their bright lights—can mesmerize many animals; approaching vehicles are all but upon them before they attempt to leap out of danger.

In areas where you might encounter animals—where woods border the highway, or signs warn of an open range or an animal habitat—reduce speed, frequently alternate your headlights from high beam to low beam (to scare animals out of the way and to prevent mesmerizing them), leave more distance between your car and the one just ahead (in case its driver brakes suddenly to avoid an animal), and, where traffic permits, hug the highway's center, giving you more room to maneuver if you spot animals ahead.

One way to spot them is to increase your peripheral vigilance: scan both sides of the road, near and far. Slow down if you can't see the road ahead, for example, on curved roads. Animals may lurk just around the bend. When you see one animal, expect others. Few animals travel alone.

Elk habitat sign alerts savvy drivers to maintain peripheral vigilance: keep your eyes scanning both sides of the road, near and far.

➤ WHAT TO DO

1. Brake fast and attempt to stop if you have enough time and there is enough distance.
2. Flick the headlights to startle the animal if it's in or near the roadway.
3. Do not take radical evasive action. Hard evasive steering can send you into a ditch, risks a head-on collision with oncoming vehicles, or, in icy or slippery weather, can put you in a skid. Evasive steering is often useless anyway. You simply don't know when or in what direction the frightened or transfixed animal will move.
4. Moments before possible impact, steer behind or ahead of the animal. You may miss it.
5. If a collision is unavoidable, steer to avoid a midsection hit. A midsection collision

Thousands of animals, domestic and wild (like this coyote), are annually involved in car collisions.

with a large animal—some deer may weigh 300 pounds, cattle twice that—may throw the animal through the windshield, endangering your life or doing serious car damage.

6. After impact there is little you can do except report the collision (required by law in some states) from the next available phone. Call the local state police or sheriff's office. To pinpoint where the collision occurred, calculate the mileage (using the car's odometer) from the point of impact to the phone location. Mileage noted, you can tell authorities, the "collision took place five miles back from where I'm phoning." Come daylight, police and/or Humane Society agents may be able to find the animal. If it is a farm animal, you may be required by law to compensate its owner. Some states require drivers to report only road-killed game animals—like deer, antelope, moose, and elk.

FREE YOURSELF
IF YOUR CAR IS SUBMERGED

It happens only in newspapers, until the unbelievable day it happens to you. Driving at night in a flood-plagued area, you drive into the water through a break in the bridge. Or, forced suddenly off the road by another car, your car heads straight into a river or lake. Or you gambled that a frozen lake was firm enough to support your car, but the ice gives way.

Some cars, on plunging into the drink, may float for a few seconds. Newer cars with unitized bodies may float for several minutes. Older cars, and especially pickup trucks and convertibles, may submerge immediately. Their heavy front ends nose down first.

Most cars will usually become submerged, even in a river that is not particularly deep or near the shoreline of a lake. Drivers submerged in shallow water can often get out of the car and to the surface if they can banish panic and concentrate.

In a submersion where the windows are closed, water may enter the car relatively slowly. If the car is upright but nose down (the heavy end lower than the rear), a large air pocket may form near the ceiling in the back. If the car is rolled on its side or upside down, the air pocket will be on its high side, whether along the former floor or to one side or the other.

Surprisingly, the electrical systems of most submerged cars continue to function, at least for a while. At night, the headlights of a submerged car are often visible from the surface. Power windows generally continue to operate, especially with the newer, sealed-type battery.

In such a situation, you may have more time and more breathing room than you might think. Still, you have no time to waste—and absolutely no time to panic. Panic robs you of your ability to do what you must to free yourself and get to the surface.

➤ WHAT TO DO

1. Free yourself from your lap and shoulder belt. If there are passengers in the car, help free them once you are free.
2. Go where the air pockets are. Breathe deeply to reduce panic and focus your mind on escaping.
3. Quickly consider your possible escape routes. The doors are useless avenues of es-

If the car becomes submerged, escape through a window.

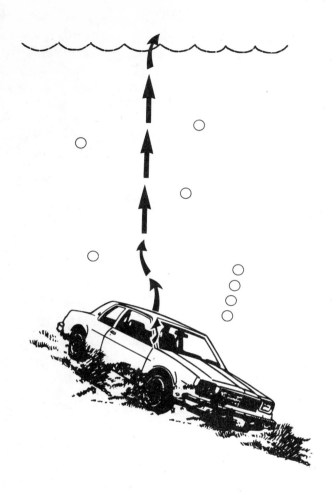

cape. Water pressure will hold them tightly shut until the pressure inside the car equals the pressure outside. This means waiting until the car is almost completely filled with water (and the air pockets flooded) before you can attempt to open the doors. You cannot afford to wait that long.

Windows, or possibly the windshield (which can sometimes pop out with a strong kick), are your best escape hatches.

4. Take a big breath, use the steering wheel as a backstop, and kick out a window (one kick may do it). Kick once or twice more, if necessary, to remove any dangerous fragments of glass.

5. If an air pocket remains, take a final big breath, slide through the window, and head for the surface. If no air remains, you have no choice but to go with what breath you

have. Once on the surface, you can take another big breath and dive down to the car (if you're a good swimmer) to help other passengers.

When you reach dry land, immediately wrap yourself and your passengers in blankets to prevent hypothermia. Get into dry, warm clothes and check into a hospital emergency room, even if you think medical attention isn't necessary. At the very least, you may be suffering from shock.

As for your car? A tow truck can usually retrieve it and a repair shop may be able to restore it to working condition—unless it was submerged in salt water. Salt water is so corrosive that few cars can be repaired once submerged in it, even if for only seconds.

A CHILD DARTS INTO YOUR PATH

It is one of the most terrifying of driving emergencies: a child suddenly darts into your path. How you react in that moment—which may be no more than a split second—depends on your driving skill and a host of variables: your distance from the child, your speed, street and weather conditions, and your car's mechanical fitness (brakes, tires).

A child's life may depend on how quickly you react. Some drivers panic. Some do what they must do. Some, not blessed with innate instant reflexes, fail to act quickly enough. Others are simply not physically able to react as fast as they must.

➤ WHAT TO DO

If a child darts out directly in your path:

1. Floor the brakes.
2. If you can't fully stop in time, swerve *behind* the child—left or right, in the opposite direction from which he or she is running.
3. If this means jumping a curb and onto a lawn, brace for it. If it means swerving into side traffic or brushing cars parked by the curb, do what you must. (Applying the brakes should slow your speed to a few miles an hour—perhaps less than 15 mph.)

If the child darts out well ahead of you:

1. Hit the brakes hard.
2. With time to maneuver, gauge the child's movements.
3. Don't sound the horn. It may cause the child to panic and backtrack.
4. Swerve hard, if you must, to steer out of the child's path—usually behind him or her.

5. In swerving, keep the car pointed ''ahead,'' to the right or left of the child's path. Avoid abrupt steering that might cause the car to broadside—to turn sideways to the direction you are steering. Broadsiding risks loss of control, a rollover, and possibly striking the child.
6. With skill and a hard stomp on the brakes you can avoid the child, with no more wear on your car than smoking tires and loss of some tire tread.

FILL A GAS TANK FROM A TOTE CAN

Running out of gas. It's downright embarrassing. Depending on road and weather circumstances, it could also prove to be something far worse. But if you are out of gas and stranded, and can manage to get to the nearest filling station, you may be able to fill a tote can with a precious gallon of gas (enough to let you drive to the station for a fill-up).

But when you get back to the car and unscrew the gas cap, ready to pour, you may discover that you can't pour gas into a gas tank from a tote can. That is, unless the tote can has one of those flexible nozzles.

Without a nozzle capable of bending or otherwise adjusting to reach into the recessed fill pipe, you won't be able to pour so much as a spoonful of gasoline into the tank. Attempt it, and all you will do is spill gasoline.

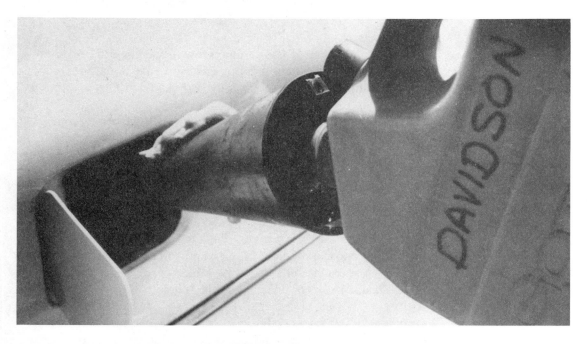

Today's gas tanks cannot be filled from a tote can unless you have a funnel.

A newspaper makes a surprisingly sturdy and efficient funnel.

➤ WHAT TO DO

1. Somehow you've got to devise a funnel, something a few inches long to bridge the gap between your tote can and the gas tank's fill pipe. If you have a long-necked funnel (some drivers carry them), the problem is solved. If you don't, you've got to create one.

   Virtually anything can be rolled to make a funnel. What works best is something sturdy—a magazine cover, lightweight cardboard, a piece of liner material from the trunk's sidewall, or even rolled newspaper. Although the latter will get soggy and leak, if you pour fast enough you can keep gasoline loss to a minimum. Whatever material you use, wrap it in several places along its length with mastic or duct tape.

2. Before attempting to fill the tank, be sure the car is level. If it's on a slope, more than a gallon may be needed to get the car going. Push the car to a level spot.

3. Insert one end of the funnel into the gasoline fill pipe and spread the other end a little to make pouring from the tote can as spill-free as possible.

4. If your funnel begins to leak before you've emptied the tote into your tank, stop and fashion a new funnel.

5. An engine that has run out of gas may need several tries—engine crankings—to get started. This is because the dry fuel pump must push fuel through the system. Each time you crank the engine, a little more fuel passes through until there's enough in the system for the engine to start.

THE DOOR SUDDENLY FLIES OPEN WHILE YOU ARE DRIVING

It may have happened to you. Moments after pulling away from the curb, the door—usually the driver-side door—flies open.

➤ WHAT TO DO

1. Make no attempt to close it if you're traveling at high speed. The airstream will fight any attempt you make to close the door. Besides, reaching may cause you to take a hand from the wheel and your eyes from the road.
2. Slow down or brake (if the road behind you is clear).
3. When you've stopped or slowed sufficiently, reach for the door handle and close it.
4. If the door opened because of a mechanical failure (relatively rare), you'll have to tie it shut until you can have the latch fixed. Actually, some apparent latch problems—those involving the external, door-end closing and locking device—involve nothing more than turning the ratchet-type, locking mechanism, if your car has one. It sometimes sticks. Turning it with a finger to a new position may solve the problem.
5. If not, tie the door shut with anything you have at hand—for example, rope, twine, or wire. Heavy duct tape may also keep it closed long enough to drive to a service station or garage.
6. Tying a door shut may be difficult if your car has recessed door handles or no "handles" at all. Still, there *is* a way to keep it shut. It involves running a length of rope around the entire door and securing the rope to a seat frame or a seat belt bracket. Another method is to open both opposite door windows and run rope through both windows and across the exterior roof. You can secure the rope with a knot tied from the driver's seat, since running the rope through the windows will prevent the opening of either. To get out, you can cut or unknot the rope from inside the car.

RESCUE SOMEONE CAUGHT IN A POWER WINDOW

"**I**t's breezy back here," your six-year-old reports from the backseat. With your eyes on the road, you reach for the switch that rolls up the rear power windows.

Suddenly your child screams in pain. His hand is caught in the closed power window. Frantically, you press the switch the other way. The window won't lower. Something has gone wrong with the mechanism.

➤ WHAT TO DO

1. If you drive a late-model luxury car, this emergency is unlikely to happen. That type of car has an emergency reverse mechanism. When the closing window encounters any resistance or pressure, it automatically reverses and begins to lower.

   Without the window reverse feature, nothing will free your child's hand but brute force. Either you've got to break the window or find something to pry the window open wide enough to free the hand.

2. Pull quickly to the shoulder or curb, put the transmission in Park, but leave the engine running.

   Keep trying to make the power switch work. Don't shut off the engine or pull the fuse that controls the window's mechanism. These measures will not lower the window.

3. You have no choice but to pry the window open, if only a fraction of an inch, despite likely damage to the window, the window frame, and the window mechanism. Your car should contain a number of items you can use to pry the window open: the tire jack's handle in the trunk, a wheel cover pried from a wheel, the metal air filter cover of older cars, even a metal ashtray yanked from the dashboard or an armrest. If you don't have any of these items, check the roadside for a piece of steel or wood.

4. With a sweater or coat, cover the trapped hand and as much of the child as you can in case the glass breaks.

5. Insert your tool as far from the trapped hand as you can. Pry the window down, using the window frame as a support. With force and enough determination, you

may be able—hopefully without breaking the glass—to force the pane down enough to free the trapped hand.

Power window gears, however, are quite strong. It is more probable that you'll break the window before breaking the gears. Most car windows don't break in jagged slices, as do home windows. They break into small, not particularly sharp pieces of glass. Even if you break the window, its pieces are unlikely to injure the child, if you've provided some protection.

PUT OUT AN ENGINE FIRE

Heavily trafficked commuter routes are daily plagued by noncollision car fires—cars not involved in accidents that suddenly, often unexplainably, catch fire. The National Highway Traffic Safety Administration (NHTSA) reports that three in every 1,000 cars on the road (more than 60,000 annually) fall victim to noncollision fires.

Some noncollision fires, says NHSTA, can be blamed on faulty or poor maintenance. Contributing factors include higher engine and exhaust temperatures in late-model cars, which have created more antifreeze and oil leak fires than ever before.

Another source of noncollision car fires are uncorrected manufacturer's defects. In 1992, NHTSA cited potential fire hazards as the reason for ordering the recall of 69,000 cars. Some of the specific reasons for these recalls included:

- An electrical short circuit can develop in a glove compartment map light and can result in a glove compartment fire.
- Aluminum fuel line fittings on certain fuel injection lines can corrode, causing the fuel line fittings to break, resulting in increased risk of fire.
- A misrouted hydraulic brake hose can become hot under certain conditions and cause the brake fluid to catch fire.
- A misalignment of a bolt may puncture the top of the fuel tank, which can result in a vehicle fire.
- A retaining clamp holding the fuel hose in the engine compartment can lose its tension and allow fuel seepage, possibly causing a fire under the hood.

Fire can strike any car, so you must be prepared for this emergency.

➤ WHAT TO DO

If a fire breaks out under the hood on a highway:

1. As smoke billows from under the hood, quickly get to the road's shoulder.
2. Switch off the ignition. Killing the engine will shut off the flow of fuel (if a fuel

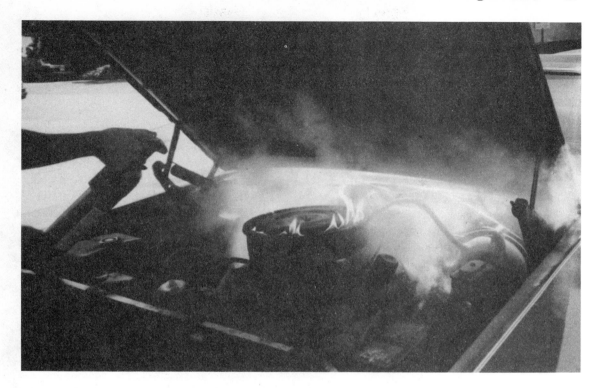

Putting out an engine fire.

line has failed) and cut off electricity to the spark plugs, another possible point of ignition.

3. Order everyone to stand clear of the car (at least 50 to 100 feet away).

4. If you have a fire extinguisher (preferably a "dry" chemical, multipurpose extinguisher with a Class B rating for flammable liquids), grab it from under the front seat or pull it free if it's clipped under the dashboard (it should not be stored in the trunk) and race to the front of the car.

5. As you head for the hood, tell any passengers to flag down other cars. Another driver may have an extinguisher, if you don't. Even if you do, two extinguishers are better than one.

6. Before lifting the hood, test its latch first. It may be hot. If hot, use a handkerchief or a rag as an insulator.

7. Throw the hood open. A quick glance should tell you whether this is a fire you can control (confined to the engine compartment) or one too far advanced for extinguishing. Many, if not most, of these fires can be quickly put out with a well-directed dousing from your extinguisher.

8. If the flames are small and confined (e.g., to the carburetor or to the place where a fuel, oil, or hydraulic fluid line has ruptured), give the area a quick, short burst from the extinguisher. Don't make the mistake of emptying the extinguisher in a frantic first try. Fuel and oil fires may flare anew after you believe they are out. Save some of the extinguisher's contents for a flare-up.

9. If you don't have an extinguisher, and if the fire seems contained to a small area of the engine compartment, you still may be able to put it out with resources you have at hand—a shovelful of roadside sand, gravel, or dirt.

10. Small fires, like carburetor fires, can often be smothered with the quick and decisive use of blankets, tent, tarp material, or almost any material closely woven and heavy enough to shut off air to the flames. You have little to lose trying. You may extinguish the fire quickly before it spreads to the rest of the car. If the fire spreads, abandon all extinguishing efforts. Quickly get well away from the burning car—a distance of at least 100 feet. If flames reach the gas tank, the car will most likely explode.

11. If you have a car telephone or CB radio, should you take the time to phone or radio for help? That depends on the fire's size, intensity, and how fast you can call for help. Sometimes, if a fire is confined to a small area (a ''spot'' fire, rather than one covering the entire engine compartment), shows no immediate signs of spreading, and cannot be extinguished, a call for help may be prudent. That's especially true if you're on a highway. A CB radio may summon a trucker to your aid (most truckers carry extinguishers).

12. Once you've extinguished the engine fire, determine whether you can make repairs (for example, wrap an oil or fuel line with duct tape) and whether it is possible or safe to drive to a service station. Flash fires under the hood often do surprisingly little actual damage—provided they are quickly extinguished. What often burns isn't electrical wiring or other flammable engine compartment parts but rather flammable oil, fuel, hydraulic fluid, or even antifreeze.

If fire breaks out under the hood in town:

Yell for someone to call the fire department or call them yourself. Whether you should attempt to douse the fire depends on the availability of an extinguisher and if the fire seems confined.

If fire breaks out from somewhere other than under the hood:

If the fire is somewhere beneath the chassis and threatens to reach the gas tank, get out fast (don't try to remove your belongings) and stand well clear of the car. Abandon any attempt to fight the fire.

COPE WITH ONCOMING HEADLIGHTS

At night many drivers are blinded by oncoming headlights and don't even know it. For a matter of seconds, an oncoming car's headlights make it impossible to see the road or what's immediately ahead. Those vision blackouts may seen inconsequential, but they can result in a sudden emergency, like a collision with an unseen animal or a skid on an unobserved patch of snow or ice.

Traveling more than 60 mph at night, you cannot afford to be blinded, even for a split second.

➤ WHAT TO DO

1. Never stare directly at oncoming headlights. Even when the lights have passed, your eyes have still not recovered their full nighttime road vision and may not for several seconds. As an oncoming car draws near, divert your eyes from its headlights. Look anywhere but directly at them. Fix your eyes on your lane only or look right—anywhere to the right of the lights, perhaps at the place where your lane and the shoulder converge or, if driving in a center lane, where your lane and the one on your right meet.
2. As lights approach, fix the image of the road in your mind. Should you become blinded, you won't outdrive your memory. You'll know if there are cars close ahead, a patch of snow, or anything else you need to be aware of immediately.
3. If an approaching vehicle is driving with its bright lights on, threatening to blind you, signal the oncoming car to switch beams by flicking your headlights from high beams to low beams. This high-low signal is understood by most drivers as a request to switch to low beams.
4. During the seconds when the lights are closest and passing, divert your attention to something in your car: turn up the radio, switch stations, or adjust your day-night driving mirror for night driving (this mutes the glare of headlights coming from behind).
5. If you become momentarily blinded, slow down. Realize that it will take several

seconds for your eyes to become accustomed to darkness again. If you have memorized the road ahead, those seconds of reduced vision should not be problematic.

6. If the glare of oncoming headlights seems unusually severe and distracting, your windshield may be dirty from tobacco smoke or, if your car upholstery or the padding on your dashboard is vinyl, from vinyl vapor (a glass-filming residue given off by vinyl in hot weather). A dirty windshield increases headlight glare. Stop at the next service station and clean the windshield, inside and out.

STAY AWAKE ON THE ROAD

You come alert with a start. You're certain you saw it—an ill-defined strange shape crossing the road just ahead. Instinctively, you brake hard. But there is nothing to brake for. You are a drowsy driver—and an accident statistic in the making.

In 1991, the National Highway Traffic Safety Administration (NHTSA) reported that of 36,895 fatal crashes, 21,889 involved only a single vehicle. Even allowing for the 38.5 percent of highway fatalities tagged ''alcohol-related,'' remaining were thousands of single-car crashes and fatalities in which a vehicle inexplicably ran off the road or hit a fixed object, such as a tree, a guardrail, or bridge.

NHTSA found that drivers in at least 1,708 fatal crashes were drowsy, asleep, fatigued, ill, or had blacked out. Drowsiness or fatigue was also a likely reason why thousands more ran

It's not only highways that hypnotize drivers into drowsiness, but also arrow-straight back roads like this.

off the road or failed to keep in the proper lane (15,244 fatal crashes), operated their vehicles erratically or recklessly (3,086 fatal crashes), or failed to yield the right of way (4,589 fatal crashes).

➤ WHAT TO DO

If you decide to stop:

1. Call it a drive and check into a motel. Some motels have special rates for "sleepers"—drivers who need just a few hours of sleep.

Douse your face with cold water.

2. Or pull into a highway rest area, a restaurant, or service station parking lot, shut off the engine, lock yourself in, and get some sleep.
3. In rest areas, particularly at night, park among other cars and trucks where rest-area users congregate. Avoid dark and remote parts of the rest area.

If you must continue driving:

1. Before setting out on a long, sleepless drive, pack some munchies: precut celery, sliced apples, sectioned oranges—invigorating fruits and vegetables you can eat without taking your eyes off the road or both hands off the wheel.
2. If you have companions, alternate drivers. Don't risk your life and those of your passengers by insisting on driving just because it's your car. While a companion drives, get some rest. Sleep if you can.
3. If you are alone on the road, roll down the windows (winter or summer) if you feel sleepy. At least one window should be rolled down all the way. An air-cooled (not air-conditioned) car can help alleviate drowsiness. Another good reason for letting in fresh air is your drowsiness might be a symptom of carbon monoxide poisoning.
4. Whether alone or not, do some simple exercises. Grasp and release the steering wheel. Reach for something, even an imaginary object. Bend and unbend an elbow.
5. Turn up the volume of your radio. Listen only to fast, rollicking music, not drowsy, slow tunes. Sing along with the music. Talk to yourself. If you have an audiobook tape, get involved in the reading. It'll energize your mind and reduce sleepiness and fatigue.
6. Stop frequently—every hour or so—at a roadside restaurant, for example. Frequent stops help segment long drives into a series of short ones.

    Don't rely solely on coffee or any other beverage containing caffeine to keep you awake. Their stimulus wears off quickly. It's more important that you eat lightly and stay away from food that's greasy. Heavy, especially greasy, food brings on drowsiness.
7. When you leave a restaurant, don't just climb back behind the wheel. Spend at least five minutes doing something in the fresh air, if only walking around the car.
8. Another tip for banishing fatigue is to pull into a rest area and jog around its perimeter a few times. Bathe your face in cold water at a drinking fountain (most rest areas have them).
9. But if you find yourself lane hopping, or braking for phantoms, give up the fight to stay awake at the wheel. Check into a motel or pull into a rest area for some sleep.

JACK UP A CAR

Automotive experts who are not always in agreement on how to deal with car and driving emergencies, agree unanimously on one point: never work under a car when it's raised off the ground on a jack. A jacked-up car is intrinsically unstable. For one thing, a car is meant to rest solidly on four wheels. For another, jacks can slip out from under a car for all manner of reasons. And car jacks do fail occasionally.

Just as there is a right way to change a tire in an emergency (see How to Change a Tire, page 185), there's a right and safe way to jack up a car to change a tire or to make any other repair that requires jacking.

➤ WHAT TO DO

1. Find a level place for jacking. This may mean driving a short distance on a flat tire. On a hill or slope, park across the incline, never in the direction of the slope.
2. Firmly set the parking brake. Put the transmission in Park or shift into a gear. Turn off the engine. Switch on your four-way hazard flashers to warn traffic that you have pulled to the road's shoulder. If you have warning reflectors or, at night, flares, put them out.
3. Before getting out the jack, consult your owner's manual for the location of your car's jacking points—the reinforced areas or fixtures under the chassis, often part of or supported by the strongest part of the car's frame near each wheel. The jacking point is designed to firmly support, engage, and fit whatever type of head (top) your jack has.
4. Follow any special jacking instructions for your car. If your car is equipped with air suspension or another type of special suspension, you must deactivate the suspension before a wheel is jacked.
5. Inspect the areas where you'll be placing the jack and its base. Is it sandy, snowy, icy, or muddy? For safe and proper jack support you may either have to remove the sand and snow from where you intend to place the jack or prepare the jacking area in some other way. One way is to find a stout board to place under the jack. Lacking that, use the car's floor or trunk mat, or even an article of clothing that will give the jack firm support.

A compact, scissors-type jack is standard equipment in many cars.

6. Even with the parking brake on and the transmission in Park or in gear, the car might still roll when one of its wheels is jacked off the ground.

    To prevent this, put a chock—a large rock, a large piece of wood, a cement block—under the opposite wheel diagonally from the one you intend to jack. When lifting a rear wheel and the car is on a slope, it is wiser to put chocks under both front wheels (see How to Block the Wheels to Prevent Roll-Away on page 109). Or you can chock all four tires. (Chocks are placed firmly under the tire treads in the direction the tire would roll.)

7. Get out the jack and jacking tools. Scissor-type jacks are raised and lowered by rotating the jack handle (or you can sometimes use a wheel wrench for a jack handle). With each rotation, the jack's head will go up (or down) a little way.

When you use a jack, your car should be on a level, solid place.

8. When you are ready to jack up the car, raise the jack until its head firmly engages its jacking point. You may need to slightly lower and raise the jack several times, each time adjusting the jack or its base until the jack seems securely placed beneath its jacking point.

9. In changing a tire, loosen all the wheel's nuts while the tire is still on the ground. Even when you do jack up the car, the tire should be only two to three inches off the ground.

   The higher a car is jacked and the higher a jack is raised, the more unstable both become. One reason many carmakers have abandoned bumper jacks is that even when the bumper is strong enough to be jacked, the jack must often be raised so high to get a wheel off the ground that the jack becomes unstable. The risk is that either the jack will slip or the car will slip off the jack. That can be exceedingly dangerous to anyone changing a tire.

10. A jack is lowered the same way you raise it, either by pumping or rotating its jack handle.

INSTALL A COMPACT SPARE TIRE

A compact spare is installed exactly like a conventional spare (see How to Change a Tire, page 185). But there are some differences worth keeping in mind when changing a compact spare (also called a ''mini,'' a ''special spare,'' a ''polyspare,'' or a ''temporal spare'').

Unlike a regular spare tire, the smaller compact spare is not designed for long mileage or for high speeds. Compacts are used just to get you going after a flat, until you can find a repair shop. The tread life—meaning tire life—of a compact is generally only about 2,000 miles. And that's pushing it. Generally, too, compacts should not be operated at speeds above 50 mph.

Install a compact spare tire exactly like a conventional tire.

Inflation pressure for compacts is usually quite high, sometimes far higher than for conventional tires. Depending on their design, some car manufacturers recommend that compacts be inflated to pressures as high as 60 pounds per square inch, double the recommended conventional inflation pressure.

A car riding on a compact also has less ground clearance than when running on four conventional tires. That's important to keep in mind in off-highway situations or even on high-center rural roads.

➤ WHAT TO DO

1. Don't install snow chains on a compact.
2. Don't exceed your vehicle's maximum load capacity (specified in your owner's manual, but sometimes also on the compact tire).
3. Don't tow a trailer while running on a compact.
4. Don't use the compact as a regular tire. Get the flat tire repaired or replaced as soon as possible, and reinstalled in place of the compact.
5. Don't use more than one compact tire on your car at a time.
6. Don't borrow a compact from another car to put on yours. Most compacts are designed to be used only with specific cars. Nor should you lend your compact to another driver to put on his or her car.
7. Don't attempt to repair a compact. Have repairs done, if at all, by a professional.
8. Don't go through an automatic car wash with a compact on.

PUT ON TIRE CHAINS

Whether you buy them or rent them, tire chains are the most unpopular automotive accessory. Most drivers hate installing them (they shouldn't be used with front-wheel-drive cars). They hate driving with them, too, because even when chains are properly fitted, they restrict speed. Some carmakers recommend you drive no more than 30 mph on tire chains. If you drive faster than that, the chains can fly off and do major damage to the body of the car. Even if they don't fly off, chains have a nasty habit of loosening and thumping the underside of fenders, and can punch right through automotive sheet metal. Chains are also rough on tires, shortening tread life and chafing sidewalls.

However, chains provide superior drive-wheel traction (only the two drive wheels are chained) in deep snow, ice, sand, and mud. In a test conducted by the National Safety Council, the traction of regular tires, conventional snow tires, and standard tires fitted with reinforced steel tire chains were measured in snow conditions. The chained tires' traction proved to be 313 percent better than the traction of standard tires and more than 250 percent better than the traction of conventional snow tires. On ice, chained tires had more than 300 percent better traction than even the traction of studded snow tires.

Other tests attest to the chains' stopping ability. Cars variously equipped with standard tires, regular and studded snow tires, and reinforced tire chains were stop-tested on glare ice. The results below indicate the distance traveled before each car stopped:

Tires	Stopping Distance (20 mph on glare ice) (in feet)
Regular tires	149
Regular snow tires	151
Studded snow tires	120
Reinforced tire chains	75

On snowy, icy roads, nothing moves unless the wheels are chained.

Whether you use link or cable tire chains, there are three basic ways to install them. (For variations, see the instructions that come with your chains.) In all cases, however, the chain's fasteners (or clasps) are fastened on the backside of the tire first, then to the outside of the tire.

➤ WHAT TO DO

1. **Drape-over method** (requires two people, a chain tender and a driver). To chain a tire with this method (you can even do both tires at the same time), stretch a chain out ahead of the tire. Pick up the farthest (front) end and drape the chain over the tire, with the chain's hooks or fasteners facing outward, and the rear of the chain just

touching the ground. Inch the car forward over the chain until what was the chain's front end moves to the rear. The chain tender then reaches around the tire and buckles the inside clasp, pulling the chain as tight as possible. (To do this, you may need to back the car up a bit.) To tighten further, the inside clasp may have to be moved to a farther link and rebuckled. This may result in a few "orphan links"—that can thump the inside of the fender when there's insufficient clearance between tire and fender—if all the links are not tied down in the final step: installing the chain tensioner. The tensioner draws together the outer edges of the chain, assuring a sustained and tight tire fit.

2. **U-clip method** (can be installed by one person). To use this method, you need a U-shaped clip wide enough to fit over the tire. You can fashion one from stiff wire or even a coat hanger. A length of rope slipped through the wheel may do as well. Lay the chain out straight behind the tire and clip or tie the front end of the chain to the tire. Drive forward and the clip (or rope tie) will pull the chain around the tire. Reach behind the tire and fasten the inside clasp, then the front clasp. That done, you can clasp and reclasp for tightness, and install the tensioner.

A wheel properly fitted with link-type chains.

3. **Cable** (as contrasted to link) **chains** (easily installed by one person). Lay the cable chains flat in front of each drive wheel, with the chains' keyhole slot fasteners (functioning as clasps) toward the front of the car.

   Pick up the chain, being careful not to twist it, and drape it over and around the tire. Use both hands and be sure the cross cables (the cross-tread cable members) are straight across the tire's tread. Then tuck the first cross cable beneath the tire. Reach behind the tire and thread the cable's end through the fastener's keyhole slot. Pull the cable tight and lock it in place with the cable lug.

   Use the same thread, tighten, and lock method on the cable's outside. Retaining clips secure any excess cable. You may need to readjust and tighten to be sure the cross cables lie straight across the tread. Drive a quarter mile or so and stop to inspect the cables. You may have to readjust and retighten them.

4. **Wood block method** (can be installed by one person). Spread the chain straight out in front of a tire. *Beneath* the chain's third and fourth cross links (between the ground and chain) place a block of wood (for example, a two-by-four). Drive the car forward on the chain until the wheel climbs and is supported by the wood block beneath the chain. Get out and pull the chain over and around the tire. Tighten the chain, then buckle the inside clasp. Tighten some more and buckle the outside clasp. Adjustments can be made easily because much of the car's weight is on the block, not solely on the chain.

If bogged down in mud:

1. Spread a chain in front of each drive wheel, with the rear edge of the chains slipped beneath the forward edge of the mired tires.
2. By shifting into low gear and driving slowly forward on the chains, you can move the car one chain-length.
3. If this doesn't get your car out of the mud trap, lay the chains down again. Again drive the car forward a chain length. Few mud holes are so large or deep that they require more than one chain application.

If bogged down in sand:

Use the same chain technique as for mud. Notice that in neither case are chains actually fitted to the drive wheels, as they would be in normal snow driving. The reason: in deep sand or mud it's all but impossible to install chains on wheels. Even jacking up the wheels to get the chains on (a dangerous practice) seldom works. A jack has no firm foothold in sand or mud.

SEPARATE LOCKED BUMPERS

Bumper lockups. They happened more frequently in the era of "chromed straights"—metal bumpers that ran straight across the front and rear of cars. But many sport trucks and vans still have them, and even today's less obtrusive bumpers still occasionally fall prey to this once common emergency.

A bumper lockup can occur if you hit the front of your car—it may not take much of a blow for your bumper to run under or over another bumper—against the back of another car. Like a couple of deer with antlers locked, the bumpers can get stuck. Backing up or attempting to pull them apart manually usually won't unlock them.

➤ WHAT TO DO

1. Decide which driver will be the "stander" and who will be the "driver."
2. If you're the "stander," stand on the lower of the two locked bumpers. Your weight should depress the bumper, lowering it slightly below the top bumper.
3. As your weight depresses the lower bumper, the driver's car can slip free. Disengaging the bumpers can be as quick and easy as that.
4. If your weight isn't enough to depress the lower bumper, try bouncing up and down on it. As your jumping depresses the lower bumper, the driver should be able to get free.

   But if the impact of your cars has pushed the bumpers into a deeper, more embracing lockup, you may have to resort to one of several other means.
5. With one method, you free the bumpers by jacking up the top one, then driving them apart. Generally, this calls for two car jacks—yours and the other driver's.

   When you jack up the end of the top bumper vehicle, use only that vehicle's "jack points." Jack points are the places on the car's chassis designated for jacking (check your owner's manual to find out where they are on your car). Most cars and light trucks should not be jack-lifted by their bumpers. Not many of today's bumpers are strong enough to be jacked up.
6. When the car with the higher bumper is raised a few inches above the other, drive the car with the lower bumper out from under the jack-raised bumper.

Sports trucks and some cars still carry bumpers that can override one another, locking.

7. Another possible remedy is to deflate the two tires, front or rear, of the car with the lower bumper. But the success of this method depends on the tire pressure of the car with the higher bumper and whether its springs will keep it elevated as the other car's bumper is lowered. You can deflate most tires to as low as 10 pounds of air and still drive a short distance at slow speed. But before inflating the tires again, have them checked to make sure their beads properly engage the wheels' rims.

AVOID A RUNAWAY TIRE

Among the deadliest (although rarest) of road emergencies is avoiding a runaway tire—a tire set free in an accident or simply broken loose from a car. But more often, the tire will come from a truck. These fast-rolling dreadnoughts can weigh more than 200 pounds. Colliding with an oncoming car, they can inflict massive damage.

Depending on how, and at what speed, tires break from axles, they can travel at astonishing speeds. Momentum keeps them rolling and gives the largest of truck tires the potential impact of a minicar. In addition, their wayward course through traffic may cause serious accidents as drivers swerve into adjacent lanes to avoid colliding with the runaways.

What takes some drivers by surprise is the ability of runaway tires to jump highway dividers, roll from one side of a highway to the other, and even roll head-on toward oncoming traffic.

On less-traveled highways, it is easy to avoid a runaway tire. Simply slow down or hit the brakes. Chances are the runaway will roll harmlessly across your path. On a busy, fast-paced highway, however, eluding a runaway tire may not be as easy.

➤ WHAT TO DO

1. As a fast-rolling tire comes at you, glance in your mirrors to size up traffic behind, in adjacent lanes, and on the shoulder. You may have to take split-second evasive action or brake hard if traffic is clear around you. Quickly gauge the runaway tire's probable path.

2. Most runaway tires travel a predictable course. They seldom weave through traffic. They tend to roll straight and fast, whether across lanes of traffic or in them. In the time you have before you must act, judge if the runaway is really a threat. If not, slow to let the tire roll by you.

3. If the tire is coming at you from a right angle, and almost sure to impact the front or side of your car, either brake hard to avoid impact or quickly floor the accelerator to get out of the tire's way.

4. If the tire is coming straight at you, take evasive, lane-changing action. Generally, you won't have to move much to avoid a head-on collision. A few feet in either direction should be sufficient.

5. If traffic doesn't permit either hard braking, floorboard acceleration, or evasive lane changing, grip the steering wheel hard (to keep control), slow down if you can, and ride out the hit.

WARN ONCOMING TRAFFIC IF YOUR CAR IS STALLED

If your car is stalled, you may need to take prompt safety measures depending on whether it stalls on the highway (putting you in danger from oncoming traffic) or off the road on the highway's shoulder.

When stalled at night or in bad visibility, you may have to act even faster to warn drivers behind you to avert the start of a chain reaction pileup. But the very act of warning oncoming traffic can entail personal danger.

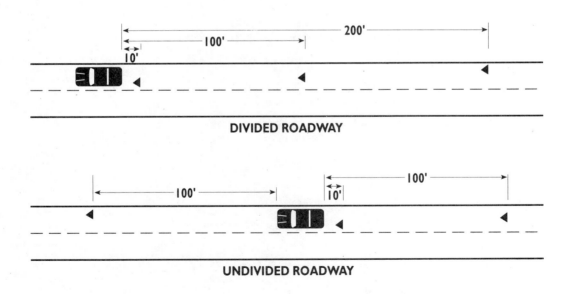

Position triangles and flares as indicated above.

➤ WHAT TO DO

1. Leave the headlights on. Switch them to automatic headlight blinking, if your car has this feature.
2. Switch on your car's hazard lights.
3. Switch on the car's inside lights.
4. Grab a flashlight and flares (which should be kept under a seat within quick reach, not locked in the trunk). On divided highways and large undivided roads, set the first flare 10 feet behind your car, in the lane where it's stalled. However, don't walk directly in the lane while you are setting up the flares. Place them on the road from the shoulder.
5. Place another flare 100 feet behind the car, then another 200 feet behind the car. In the situation you face, set as many flares as you have and as far behind your car as necessary considering traffic and weather conditions.

    On an undivided road, position one flare 100 feet in front of the car, another 100 feet behind, and a third 10 feet behind the car. If you have a driving companion, both of you should be setting flares or signaling drivers to slow down.

Best daytime road distress signals (in order of effectiveness)

1. Raise the car hood.
2. Use your car's hazard lights.
3. Set up reflective devices.
4. Light flares.
5. Attach something white to your car's antenna or traffic-side door handle.

Best nighttime road distress signals (in order of effectiveness)

1. Set up reflective devices.
2. Light flares.
3. Use your car's hazard lights.
4. Set your headlights to flash on and off, if your car has this feature.
5. Wave a powerful flashlight in a circular motion as cars approach.

To warn oncoming traffic that you are stalled, turn on the car's lights and put out triangles or flares.

In a dire emergency you might get attention and help by burning something (in a metal wheel cover, for example). Virtually anything combustible will do: rags, paper, even wood, sprinkled with oil dripped from your engine oil dipstick or doused with gasoline siphoned from the gas tank. Distress fires should be set on the road's shoulder, well away from combustible underbrush or trees. To avoid igniting a roadside fire, don't set a distress fire if it is windy.

In a driving emergency, whether in daytime or after dark, you won't go wrong using as many emergency warning devices as you have or can quickly devise.

Once deployed, a triangle should stand up to gusts of wind and vibrations from passing cars.

YOUR CAR STALLS IN THE LEFT LANE

Most highway commuters have seen cars stalled on the road. But have you asked yourself how would you deal with the emergency if you were stalled?

What actions should you take to warn oncoming traffic of your breakdown, so as to avoid a rear-ending? Having warned traffic, should you return to your car to wait for a passing tow truck or police car to get you out of traffic? Should you ever attempt, even with the help of other drivers, to push your car to the shoulder? Should you risk a dash for the shoulder and leave your car where it is stalled? Or should you, having warned traffic as best you could, get back behind the wheel and sit out a rescue if you are stalled in the left lane?

➤ WHAT TO DO

Getting to the shoulder in daylight

1. If you sense your car is stalling, fasten your seat belt (or if loose, pull it tighter). Make a quick decision: considering your car's present speed and the traffic in adjacent lanes, do you have the momentum and the time to get to either road shoulder?
2. If, after you check your rearview and sideview mirrors, you judge your car's momentum enough to make the shoulder, switch on the appropriate turn signal, blare your horn, and steer for the shoulder. To conserve momentum, quickly shift into neutral.
3. Once on the shoulder, turn on the hazard flashers (even if your engine is dead, they can operate several hours on a good battery). Turn on the headlights—even during the day. Daytime headlights can alert patrolling tow trucks or police in the highway's opposite lanes that there's a motorist in trouble. At the first opportunity they can exit, get on your side of the highway, and pull up to help you.

    Set your car's automatic headlight flashers (if you have this feature). You can't keep your headlights on too long without running down the battery, but 10 minutes may be long enough to bring help.
4. Get out and attach a flag to your car's raised antenna.
5. Lock yourself in, with windows closed up tight, and your seat belt fastened. Even on the shoulder, your car may still be rear-ended.

103

6. If you have a cellular phone, dial 911 or your auto club for help. If you don't have a phone, you may not want to risk trying to find an emergency call box. Many experts advise against it.

    Even if you've pulled to the left shoulder and there's a call box just across the highway, never risk crossing the road. At the speed cars travel, it may be difficult to judge closing distances.

If you can't make the shoulder in daylight:

1. If your car is stalling and you know you can't pull to either shoulder, you've got to act and think fast to warn traffic behind you.
2. Quickly press the brakes lightly, on-again, off-again, not to slow or stop, but to warn the driver immediately behind that you're slowing.
3. Quickly signal your intention to stop by switching on your hazard flashers.
4. Also use a hand signal. Thrust your left hand out of the driver-side window.
5. Steer to stay in your lane. Some drivers who stall in the left lane panic as they start to lose momentum and wander into adjacent lanes. That's an invitation to be side-swiped.
6. When your car stops, do not open the door. Reject the advice you've heard about getting out for a look under the hood. The left lane is no place for repairs—even if you're a driveway mechanic.
7. If you have a car phone or radio, call for help. If you don't, and if you break down on a busy highway, it is possible that someone with a car phone has already alerted authorities.
8. Sit there, with your seat belt on, and your door locked until help arrives.

HOW TO

STEER OUT OF A SKID

As you head too fast into a curve on a snowy or icy highway, the front wheels suddenly don't respond to your steering. Skidding, the car goes straight. Unless you quickly bring it under control, you'll go off the road. The car is in a *cornering* or *steering* skid. Speed or steering too abruptly has caused the front wheels to lose traction—and contact—with the slick roadway.

Or, on an oily, rain-wet pavement, you brake hard to avoid hitting a car ahead. Suddenly your car's rear begins to slip sideways. If you don't take instant corrective action, the car may spin completely around. You're caught in a *braking skid*.

Or, on a slick pavement, whether already in motion or just starting out, the car fishtails—its rear whips back and forth. Applying too heavy and too quick a foot on the throttle has put your car into an *acceleration skid*. Unless it's instantly corrected, you may collide with other cars or a structure.

These are three—*cornering/steering, braking,* and *acceleration*—types of skids you may face. They may affect just the drive wheels (whether front or rear), the steering wheel, or the car's four wheels when all are locked (no wheel is rolling).

The way to control a skid is to keep the wheels rolling (something antilock braking is designed to do). With rolling wheels, you have a chance to bring the skid under quick control. Panic braking locks the wheels (except if you have antilock brakes), preventing them from rolling.

➤ **WHAT TO DO**

1. Take your foot off the gas pedal.
2. Do not brake (during a skid's initial seconds).
3. Do not downshift.
4. Steer in the direction of the skid (with your foot off the gas), then *begin* to counter-steer.
5. Do not steer abruptly. Attempt no radical, precipitous steering.
6. As you feel the rolling wheels begin to regain traction (you are beginning to control the skid), jab the brakes quickly on and off—"squeeze-braking."
7. Continue countersteering.

105

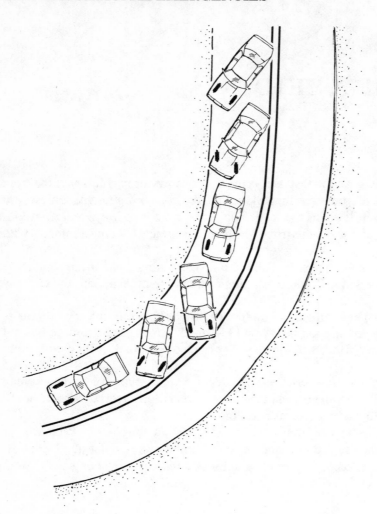

To steer out of a skid, steer in the direction of the skid.

8. With the car's speed greatly reduced (your foot has been off the gas pedal since the skid began), continue jabbing the brakes on (but not for too long) and off.
9. As the car grows more responsive to straightening, try quick, very easy acceleration. A little gentle acceleration may bring you out of the skid. If it doesn't, or if it worsens the skid, don't apply any more gas until squeeze-braking and gentle counter-steering have all but corrected the skid.
10. With the skid controlled, maintain a reduced speed.

CUSHION YOURSELF IN A COLLISION

In fast traffic, the car ahead of you suddenly stops dead. Or you see (too late) that traffic ahead is stopped. In your mind, a single word flashes: stop! But you can't stop, and you know it. There simply isn't enough braking distance. With cars on your left and right, there's no chance of a quick lane change or even a skillful maneuver that will avoid a collision: you're going to hit the car stopped ahead.

➤ WHAT TO DO

In a short-distance situation:

1. Brake fast and as hard as you can.
2. Downshift, if you can, to get a braking assist from the engine.
3. Prepare for the impact. Don't hit the car straight on. Moments from impact, steer as far left or right as you safely can (considering the traffic around you). If there is a point to aim for, it is the outer edge (either side) of the stopped car's rear bumper.

     Fast braking and calculated steering should cushion the impact. With luck, no major mechanical damage will be done to the stopped car or your car.

In a longer-distance situation:

1. With greater distance between cars, you have a chance to maneuver enough to avoid a rear-end collision altogether.
2. Braking to a stop may be impossible considering your speed and the closing distance, so brake to slow your speed as much as you can.
3. In the moments before impact, survey your options. Is there a wide shoulder, a grassy boulevard strip, or an adjacent lane you can quickly move into? Quickly pick the most promising option and steer for it. In a cloud of dust you may come to a stop on the shoulder, vault onto the divider strip, or with brakes squealing and horns sounding behind you, manage to squeeze into an adjacent lane.

     With decisive action and great skill, you can manage to avoid the seemingly unavoidable: a crunching, possibly lethal, rear-end collision.

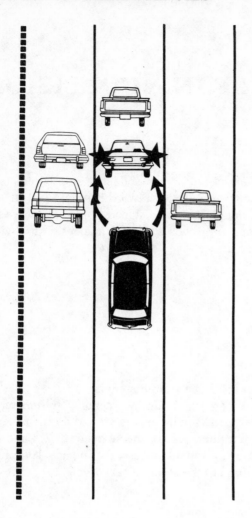

To cushion the impact when hitting a stopped car, aim for the outer edges.

BLOCK WHEELS
TO PREVENT ROLL-AWAY

Blocking or "chocking" the wheels gives you a third brake—besides the transmission or gears and your car's parking brake (which brakes only two wheels, usually the rear)—when you need to secure a car in place. You might need to block the wheels when:

- You jack up a wheel to change a tire. Depending on which wheel you lift from the ground, you have effectively lost that wheel's (and likely its partner's) braking ability. Even though you have put the automatic transmission in Park, or the manual shift in gear, the car is not as secure as it was on the ground. You block a wheel to prevent the car from rolling and slipping off the jack.
- You try to get a wheel unstuck. Attempting to drive out of mud, snow, or sand, you block the free wheels while you try to free the stuck wheels. Blocking prevents the bogged wheels from slipping back.
- Parked on a slope, you want braking insurance. In addition to setting the hand brake, putting the automatic transmission in Park, or the manual shift into gear, and turning the front wheels into the curb on a downhill grade or away from the curb on an uphill grade, you might consider blocking the wheels.
- You jack up the car to put on snow chains. Jacking a car up is one way to install tire chains. You block the wheels for the same reason you block them when jacking up a car to change a tire.
- You want to put the car on jack stands. Jack stands don't lift a car but rather support it when you need to work under the car. You jack up the car and slip jack stands under its frame or axles. To do so, the car must usually be jacked higher than when you change a tire. Blocking the wheels prevents the car from slipping off the raised jack.
- You're parked on a particularly slick or icy slope. Parked on a slick grade, blocking the wheels gives greater braking security.
- You transport your car on a ferryboat. If the boat crew does not block your car wheels, you should do so. Also, block them when your car is being transported on a flatbed truck.

But it is in an emergency—when you jack up a wheel or are stalled on a slope—where blocking is essential in preventing a rollaway. To block you simply put something—a com-

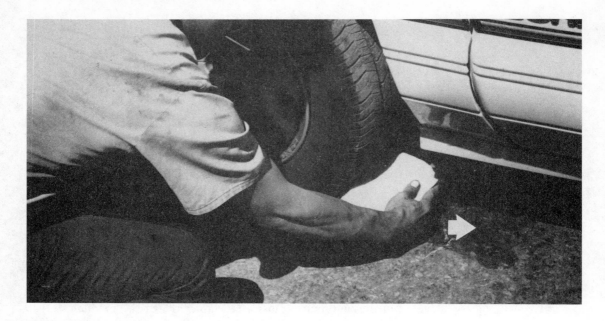

Wheels are blocked in the direction the car might roll. The arrow shows the direction of the possible roll.

mercially made metal chock (usually sold in pairs in auto supply stores), a piece of heavy timber, a large rock—behind or in front of a wheel to prevent the car from rolling forward or backward.

You can block every wheel that's on the ground or block only one or two strategic wheels. In strategic blocking, you block the wheel diagonally opposite the one you've jacked up. Jack up the front left wheel and block the rear right wheel. But block both front wheels if you're jacking up the rear of the car.

➤ WHAT TO DO

1. Determine which wheel or wheels you want to block. In inching trapped rear wheels out of mud, snow, or sand, block the car's free wheels—the front wheels—against rollback. If on a slippery or snowy grade, block them all if you have enough blocks.
2. If you don't have chocks, then find something that serves almost as well. Almost anything that will engage the treads of the tires will do. Blocking material works best if it's square-edged rather than round. (Tire treads can get a grip on a square-edged chock, but they might roll over a rounded one.) A round, ⅔-inch-diameter tree limb,

for example, might fail to adequately block a wheel where a square-edged two-by-four might do just fine.

3. Test whether your makeshift blocks will prevent the car from rolling. Release the hand brake, disengage the gears, ease off the foot brake, and let the car roll a few inches until the tires engage. If it holds, you've got effective blocks.

AVOID ROAD DEBRIS AT HIGH SPEED

Tuned to a local radio station, you hear what can only be called a debris report: "A mattress is reported across both lanes of U.S. 50, a mile east of town," or "Somebody has lost a refrigerator on I-80 near the Willow Street exit," or "A truck has spilled a load of watermelons on I-70 one mile west of the State Route 127 exit."

Maybe you smile complacently, envisioning debris cluttering the highway. Who could lose a refrigerator and not miss it? Or a mattress? As for a spilled truckload, that's more understandable. Inexplicably, however, some people are intentionally using major roads as trash dumps. They have become the new depositories for everything from produce to furniture.

As a result, drivers are meeting debris head-on on an everyday basis. Even forewarned by traffic alerts, drivers confronted by debris in their path often must gamble. Roll over it? Swerve around it? Hit it head-on? Risk braking in fast traffic? The appropriate action will depend on what kind of debris is in your path.

A cardboard box, for example, can easily be rolled over or pushed aside, unless the box is full of heavy material. Such a box can damage, even wreck, a car.

Other debris can be quickly judged harmless. Driving across the plains or deserts of the Western states, drivers often encounter tumbleweeds as tall as a small car's hood. Although you can drive through them safely, tumbleweeds do, however, have a penchant for lodging under the chassis, which means stopping to remove them.

The danger of debris on the highways is the damage it can inflict on a car and driver. Roadway debris can puncture tires, punch holes through the radiator, knock out headlights, smash a windshield, or throw a car out of control. And if the debris is slippery, like diesel fuel—a common spill—or a load of ripe vegetables, it can send you into a skid.

➤ WHAT TO DO

1. Brake, if traffic permits.
2. Usually, you don't have the choice of braking. Either you've got to swerve around whatever it is, hit it a glancing blow, or roll over it.
3. If the debris is slippery—diesel fuel or squishy vegetables—don't brake. Don't accelerate. Don't attempt to swerve around the spill. Hold your course. Maintain your present speed and drive through, even if there are crates on the road. Braking will

To cope with road debris at high speeds, swerve or hit it glancingly.

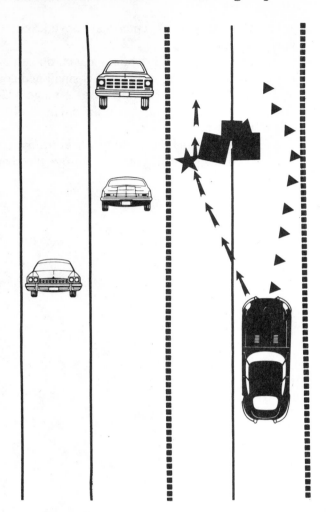

almost certainly send you into a skid. Maintaining speed should get you through with little more than splattered tires. Continue driving, without braking, until the tires have dried.

4. If what's in the road is massive—for example, a refrigerator or a piece of furniture—you face a double danger: braking to avoid the debris risks a rear-end collision, but swerving to avoid it may put you at risk for a collision with cars beside you. Hitting such massive debris almost certainly means car damage or worse.

   With a quick glance at traffic, swerve quickly around the massive obstacle. Depending on your driving skill and quick responses, you may be able to move into an adjacent lane and, once past the debris, move back without damaging your car.

5. If hitting a large object is inevitable, try to strike it a glancing blow; never hit it

head-on. Striking it off-center may move it out of your way with only bumper or fender damage.

6. Confronting "mystery" debris—that cardboard box that may be empty or full— means rolling the dice. If the box is small and compact, you might consider driving right over it. Win the gamble and no damage is done. Lose, and the debris may rip through the oil pan (reservoir of the engine's oil), put your car in the shop, and send you to the hospital.

But by grasping the steering wheel firmly to retain control and slowing down as much as you safely can, you can improve the chances of avoiding any damage.

YOU'RE FORCED OFF THE ROAD

You're driving 55 mph in heavy traffic on a two-lane highway when a car tries to pass you but is forced back into your lane because of oncoming traffic, or a car coming from the other direction straddles your lane. To prevent a collision, you steer as far right as you can. Moments later you're riding the shoulder, your left wheels on the pavement, your right wheels on the shoulder's dirt, asphalt, or concrete. You've been forced off the road.

If the shoulder is concrete, like the highway itself, you should be able to maintain control fairly easily, provided there isn't an obstacle, like a signpost, planted ahead. If the shoulder is asphalt, the car may bump along as though on cobblestones.

If the shoulder is "soft"—dirt, sand, or another unstable material—you're in big trouble: the car may fishtail, skid, or nosedive, even pitch into a possible rollover. If you're on dirt, a cloud may be plowed up by your right wheels and perilously reduce vision ahead. You may be a split-second from losing control.

➤ WHAT TO DO

1. Take your foot off the accelerator but don't brake. Braking or accelerating may compound the emergency, even throwing the car out of control and possibly causing it to jump back into traffic.
2. If skidding, steer tentatively in the direction of the skid.
3. With the skid corrected, bring the car back parallel to the highway, even though half of your wheels may still be on the shoulder.
4. Steer straight with your foot still off the gas and the car slowing down until you've regained control.
5. Still rolling, but not yet stopped, make a quick decision to steer completely onto the shoulder and stop before attempting to regain the highway, or nudge the car back onto the highway without stopping.
6. If your decision is to ride the shoulder and stop, brake lightly to a stop. Cautious braking is especially important if the shoulder is slick (muddy or slushy from rain or snow) or noticeably soft (a potential sand trap).
7. If your decision is to regain the highway, do so gradually, with a small, tentative

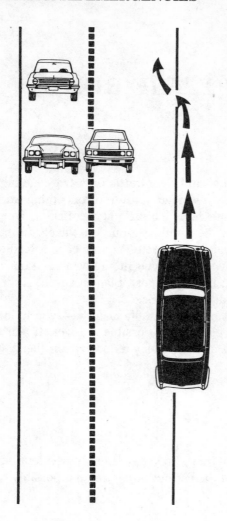

Drive on the shoulder if you're forced off the road at high speed.

turn of the steering wheel to the left. You've got to allow time for the tires on the shoulder to regain traction.

If the shoulder is lower than the highway, steering back onto the road requires more care. If the tires on the shoulder straddle the demarcation between shoulder and highway, the steering wheel can gyrate wildly. Keep control with a firm but flexible steering grip.

8. Rather than test your steering skills when run off the road, the wisest move may be to ride the shoulder, slow down, and stop (assuming the shoulder is clear of obstacles). Then get back into traffic.

YOU SUDDENLY FEEL FAINT

Driving alone on a distant highway, you suddenly feel faint. Faintness may be part of your medical history, or this may be your first serious experience, or you may be suffering from unsuspected carbon monoxide poisoning. Either way, you must get off the road and out of traffic. Faintness can sap your driving alertness and can lead, more quickly than you may anticipate, to full or partial loss of consciousness.

➤ WHAT TO DO

1. Take a few deep breaths.
2. While still driving, bend over the steering wheel as far and as low as you can without obstructing your view of the road or ability to drive. Putting your head low often wards off dizziness.
3. Get to the shoulder and stop. Put the transmission in Park or the shift in gear, shut off the engine, and, while you have the strength to do it, open all the car's windows and doors.
4. Loosen any tight or restrictive clothing—necktie, buttoned-up blouse, belt. Remove your shoes.
5. If you have medication for fainting symptoms, take it.
6. Lie down across the front seat (backseat if the car has bucket seats up front) with your head hanging over one end of the seat and your legs raised above the opposite end (supported by the door's window frame).
7. If you have water in the car, wet a handkerchief and bathe your face with it. If you don't have water, use any liquid that will help you feel cool.
8. Most faint drivers respond quickly to this simple regimen. If you believe your faintness is more than transitory, or may have been caused by carbon monoxide, drive to an emergency medical facility to see a physician. If you suspect carbon monoxide poisoning, have the car's exhaust system checked for leaks.

If you suddenly feel faint, pull off the road and open all the doors and windows. It could be carbon monoxide poisoning.

SOMETHING SHATTERS
OR OPAQUES THE WINDSHIELD

You see something on the road ahead, but you can't stop, much less slow down, to avoid it. Or, maybe from nowhere, a rock crashes against the windshield, or a violent windstorm slams debris into the windshield. The object crashes into your windshield, shatters the pane, all but obliterating your vision ahead. You're driving practically blind.

➤ WHAT TO DO

1. Don't panic.
2. Get your foot off the gas and onto the brake.
3. As you slow down, look for a spot you can see through, perhaps a small area on the driver's side of the glass.

   Today's windshields are a sandwich of multiple layers of glass with plastic film between. Usually, there's enough unaffected glass—if only a few square inches—to give you a view to steer by and allow you to slow down enough so that you can move to the shoulder (after signaling) and stop.

   Although no two windshields crack the same way, depending on where they are struck, what hits them, and at what impact, rarely is the glass totally opaqued.
4. If you absolutely cannot find a spot you can see through, quickly roll down the driver-side window, firmly grip the steering wheel, and lean far enough out to be able to see the way ahead.

YOUR UNMANNED CAR BEGINS TO ROLL

It has happened—or threatened to happen—to every car owner: you leave the shift in neutral and your car begins rolling down a slope without a driver. Whether it rolls forward or backward, a driverless "roller" can not only dent another car's fender, it can maim and kill if it rolls into traffic.

Your car can roll if you neglect to put its automatic transmission in Park or its shift in gear. It can roll if you forget to set the parking brake or don't crimp the wheels into the curb when you park on a slope. A car not securely parked can be set into motion if struck by another car.

Mechanical problems can also start a car rolling. Ailing automatic transmissions sometimes slip from Park into a gear with less hold.

Catching a runaway car depends on a number of factors: how close you are to the car as it begins to roll, how fast it is rolling, weather conditions (in the attempt to catch it you may slip and fall on snow or ice), and whether the driver-side door is open.

The risk of bodily injury in attempting to stop a rolling car is considerable. Bodily risk aside, stopping a runaway requires instant action, fast and sure footwork, agility, and luck.

➤ WHAT TO DO

1. Race to the rolling car.
2. Fling open the driver-side door.
3. Jump in and get a hand on the steering wheel and a foot on the brake pedal. (It may be easier to grab the hand brake.)
4. Once you are behind the wheel, you probably won't have the advantage of power steering or power braking (because there likely won't be time to turn on the engine), so you will need considerable strength to steer the rolling car out of trouble and bring it to a halt.

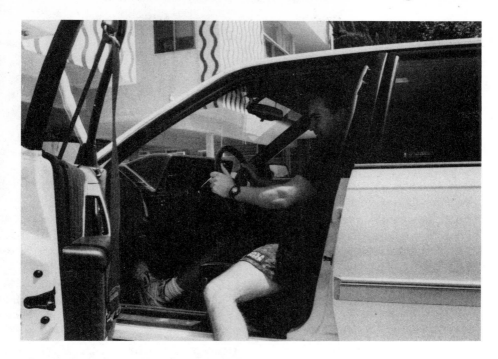

If a car begins rolling, get behind the wheel and hit the brakes hard.

YOUR CAR BEGINS TO HYDROPLANE

The highway is rain-soaked and full of puddles when suddenly the car begins to swerve, then skid. Your car is hydroplaning.

Hydroplaning can happen at almost any speed, but it is far more likely to happen at high speeds. Invariably, hydroplaning catches drivers by surprise. Inexplicably, the car begins to skid although you haven't swerved, haven't braked, haven't changed lanes, or drastically changed speed.

Yet now you are in a skid you can't seem to correct. Steering in the direction of the skid (as most driving experts advise) doesn't correct the skid or restore your control. Neither does any other quick maneuver.

If you could peer beneath the tires, you'd understand what is wrong. The tires aren't gripping the pavement. They aren't even in contact with the roadway. Or, if they are, their contact is intermittent. They are riding on a thin layer of water much as a hydroplane boat rides on water. This explains why steering won't correct the skid.

Hydroplaning is different from ordinary skidding. At high speed on a wet or oily road you may hydroplane and not know it until you attempt to slow down, turn, move to pass, or if you get hit by a gust of wind.

Hydroplaning is usually caused by worn, all-but-treadless tires, especially front tires (although it can happen with new tires as well). If you examine a new tire, you'll see that it is designed with deep channels, meant to provide an escape route for water trapped beneath the tire. When treads are badly worn, water can build up beneath the tires (with no way to escape) and literally lift them off the driving surface, if only a fraction of an inch. Without contact with the road, the car goes out of control. (To prevent hydroplaning in wet weather, tire treads should be at least one-sixteenth of an inch deep and the tires inflated to near-maximum pressure. For most tires, that's from 32 to 36 pounds per square inch.)

➤ **WHAT TO DO**

1. Take your foot off the gas pedal. Don't brake. Let the car slow down gradually.
2. Steer straight, no matter in what direction the car is momentarily skidding.

A tire's deep channels provide escape routes for water trapped beneath the treads.

3. Hold the steering wheel firmly, anticipating the moment when the tires will grip the pavement again. When that happens, the car is apt to swerve.
4. With the car no longer hydroplaning, reduce your speed. Drive slowly to a service station for a look at your tires. Chances are the treads are badly worn. You'll probably need at least two new tires.

YOU'RE GOING TO BE REAR-ENDED

Stopped at a light or at a highway exit or entrance ramp behind other cars, you glance into the rearview mirror and go numb. A car is bearing down fast. It's going to rear-end you, going to plow into the back of your car at 40 mph, perhaps far faster. And you can't escape. There's no way to prevent the hit, no way to escape being rear-ended.

In few other driving emergencies does a driver feel more helpless. With nowhere to go, you can only await the inevitable impact. There's no time, nor would it likely be prudent, to fling yourself from the car. Endangered as you are in that instant before grinding impact, you might be in greater bodily danger in the roadway, beside your car.

In a rear-end collision, you want your car, not your body, to take the brunt of the impact. To minimize possible injuries, you've got to let your seat and seatback act as a shock absorber.

➤ WHAT TO DO

1. Quickly, pull your safety belt tight.
2. Release your foot from the brake. Put the transmission in Neutral.
3. If you're not wearing your seat belt, throw yourself facedown on the floor as protection against flying glass. Rear seat passengers should do the same.
4. If you are wearing your seat belt, cover your face with your hands. Better, use anything that can protect your face and help to soften the shock: a blanket, a pillow, or clothing.
5. Still in your seat belt, get as low in the seat as you can.
6. Go limp. It can help reduce your body's absorption of impact forces. Going limp may also prevent a whiplash injury (when the head of a seated crash victim is snapped violently backward).

   With luck, and knowledge of impact preparedness, you (but probably not your car) will survive the accident without serious injury.

AVOID BEING CARJACKED

Simple, commonsense precautions—most of them obvious to any car owner—can minimize the risk of carjacking, perhaps the most feared of car crimes.

According to Maryland's Department of Public Safety and its Community Crime Prevention Institute, "the 4 A's" for reducing the risk of carjacking are:

➤ AWARENESS

- Be aware of your surroundings.
- Know your route. Use well-lighted and well-traveled roads.
- Plan ahead. Be prepared. Have an alternate route in mind in case of problems.
- Don't drive alone, if at all possible.
- Don't walk aimlessly toward your car. Walk with a purpose. The aimless driver emboldens carjackers.
- Be aware of followers—anyone who may be following you to your car.
- Be aware of "bump and rob" techniques. If you are bumped by another car, don't get out of your car unless other people are around. Even then, use caution; be suspicious.
- Recognize and be aware that carjacking can occur anytime, anywhere, and in any neighborhood.
- Be aware that any car may be the target of carjackers, not just expensive, high-profile cars.

➤ ALERTNESS

- Be alert to any activity near your car.
- Be alert to people loitering in your parking area.
- Be suspicious of people approaching your car asking for directions or change, or giving out flyers.
- Check door handles, locks, and the backseat before entering your car. Always give it a quick visual inspection for tampering. If you think someone has tampered with your car, don't enter it. Call the police, or have a friend or neighbor with you when you do enter.

- When stopped in traffic, leave enough distance between your car and the one ahead so you can pull away quickly, if necessary.
- Be alert to danger when approaching or using a drive-up automatic teller machine (ATM). Avoid using ATMs at night, especially if you see loiterers nearby.

➤ AVOIDANCE

- You'll be safer if you avoid certain risky situations.
- Never leave keys in the ignition or the engine running for any reason—even for a minute.
- Before you drive, lock all doors and close all windows.
- Don't park in secluded, poorly lighted areas, especially at night. Wherever you park, be alert to possible hiding places.
- Don't walk alone to your car, especially at night. Remember that men and women are equally vulnerable to carjacking. Walk in pairs (with a friend, companion, or business acquaintance) whenever possible.
- Have your key ready for quick car access. Don't stand by your locked car fumbling for the key. Have the key in hand, ready to quickly unlock and enter your car.
- Don't get out of your car if you see suspicious people approaching. If in doubt, drive away.
- Don't allow your car to run out of gas. Avoid gassing up at night in dimly lit or deserted gas stations, especially the self-service kind. Day or night, when gassing up, take your keys out of the ignition. Once back in the car, lock the doors and close the windows.
- To avoid home or office thefts, which sometimes follow a carjacking, detach—and carry separately—your car keys and your home and office keys. If your house or office keys are taken, immediately have the locks changed (that very day or night; it is cheap insurance). Don't leave your car registration or anything else with your home address in the car; carry the car's registration in your billfold or purse.
- If you think someone is following you, never drive home. Drive to a public place and call police. If you are sure you're being followed, drive directly to a police or fire station.

➤ ACTIONS

- If someone demands your car keys, don't resist. Comply immediately with the carjacker's demands. Resisting is dangerous and risks personal harm. Your car can be replaced, but not your life.
- If someone asks for assistance (especially at night or in an unfamiliar place), don't get out of your car. If you decide to give assistance, beckon the other driver to follow you to a safe place—like the nearest police station.
- At night, if someone approaches your car, turn on your headlights and sound the horn continuously.

- If stopped in traffic, and you believe you are in serious danger of a carjacking or robbery, run a stop sign or red light if the way is clear and if doing so distances you from a possible confrontation. At night, drive to a public, well-lighted place (like an all-night business) and call police immediately.
- Carry a pen and notebook for jotting down license numbers and descriptions of suspects and their vehicles. Don't trust such key facts to memory.

HOW TO

ELUDE AN UNWANTED FOLLOWER

For blocks you suspect it. As you purposely turn a corner or head for a highway exit ramp, you are more sure than ever. A car is following your car.

➤ WHAT TO DO

1. Don't let the follower know you are aware you're being followed. Do nothing to arouse his or her suspicions.
2. Do not drive home. Do not stop (other than for traffic lights). Do not park. Continue driving, keeping as far ahead of the follower as possible, several car lengths ahead (at the very least).
3. Do not speed up or attempt to outrun the follower. This may worsen matters.
4. Never try to elude a follower by suddenly turning corners, dodging in and out of parking lots, or making U-turns.
5. If a car appears to be following you, drive to the nearest police or fire station. If that isn't possible, drive to a lighted service station or supermarket and telephone the police. If you can't reach a safe place, stop at a location where there are people, and let the car pass you. Try to get the license number, and note the appearance of both the car and its occupants.

   If a car follows you to your driveway at night, stay in your car with the doors locked. Don't get out unless you can determine that the individual has a legitimate purpose. If necessary, sound your horn to alert your neighbors. The noise also may frighten your pursuer away.

CORRECT A SWAY OR JACKKNIFE

If you tow a trailer, a boat, or anything else, jackknifing can result if the trailer sways—does not track straight behind the tow vehicle. In extreme jackknifing, the trailer can move at almost a right angle to the tow vehicle. If the trailer is heavy enough, it can topple its tow vehicle, whether it be a car, a sports truck, a camper, or even a motor home.

Aside from your tow vehicle's standard brakes, which should also operate the trailer's brakes, you need to have a separate braking system that allows you to brake the swaying or jackknifing trailer independently of your brakes. If you don't have independent trailer brakes, which are applied manually from the tow vehicle, you are not fully prepared if your car sways and jackknifes.

With an independent trailer braking system, swaying and jackknifing are often quickly and easily controlled by applying brakes only to the trailer. Usually a few quick brake applications slow the trailer (in respect to the tow vehicle) and get it tracking straight again.

If the trailer does not have independent brakes, jackknifing may still be corrected quickly, although not with the same surety. The techniques for correcting swaying or jackknifing in a trailer with independent brakes and one without independent brakes are radically different. If the trailer has independent brakes, you can hold it back by braking it, bringing it again in line with your tow vehicle. If it doesn't have independent brakes, you can accelerate the tow vehicle to pull the trailer in line.

➤ **WHAT TO DO**

If you have independent trailer brakes:

1. The moment you're aware that the trailer is swaying or threatening to jackknife, lift your foot from your vehicle's gas pedal.
2. Don't brake the vehicle. Let both vehicles slow.
3. With a quick jab, apply the brakes to the trailer only.
4. This should straighten the trailer's track. If not, apply the trailer-only brakes again with a quick, short application.
5. With the trailer again tracking straight behind, let the vehicles slow. If necessary,

129

pull to the shoulder to investigate why the trailer swayed or threatened to jackknife. The trailer may be incorrectly loaded, the hitch's sway control may need adjustment, or road winds may be too strong for control at the speed you were traveling. If there is one universal prevention for swaying or jackknifing, it is reduced speed.

If you don't have independent trailer brakes:

1. As the trailer you're pulling jackknifes (pushing your vehicle's tail end into a skid), release all brakes, including the trailer's brakes.
2. Steer in the direction opposite the one the rear end of your car is skidding or being pushed toward.
3. Simultaneously accelerate to pull the trailer forward, forcing it to regain track and respond to your tow vehicle.
4. As the trailer begins to respond to towing and moves in line with your tow vehicle, steer in the direction you want to go.

   The quickly applied combination—brake release, countersteering, acceleration, and steering in the direction you want to go—should correct the jackknife.

WHAT TO DO IF

YOU SUSPECT CARBON MONOXIDE POISONING

Annually, accidents involving only one car account for an estimated one-third of highway fatalities—when drivers inexplicably drive off the road, swerve suddenly into highway dividers, or, apparently rested and wide-awake, fall asleep at the wheel. Why?

Some researchers point a finger at carbon monoxide—the odorless, colorless, tasteless, and silent killer that lurks in every car's exhaust (one of the products of engine combustion) as a prime suspect. Carbon monoxide can come from the exhaust of the car just ahead (through your car's intake air vents) or, more often, from your own engine and its tailpipe. Any break or leak in your car's exhaust system can infiltrate carbon monoxide into your car. "Chassis seepage" is but one way carbon monoxide can invade your car. Another is the "vacuum effect," which occurs when you crack a side window or leave your station wagon's rear window open, unknowingly creating a vacuum that pulls your own exhaust into the car.

Several years ago during winter in Vermont, state police flagged down 114 drivers and found that carbon monoxide was detectible in 12 percent of the vehicles (windows were shut, heaters on full-blast) and that carbon monoxide contamination inside the car was at the "danger" level in 4 percent.

In California, a similar road check found that 30 out of 1,007 vehicles stopped (about 3 percent) were so heavily contaminated with carbon monoxide as to impair driver alertness. Significantly, some carbon monoxide was detected in almost every one of those vehicles (cars and trucks alike).

Carbon monoxide is so insidious because of the way it attacks—and affects—the human body. Your blood has a 300-times greater preference for carbon monoxide than for life-sustaining oxygen. Given the choice—oxygen or carbon monoxide—blood absorbs far more carbon monoxide.

The symptoms of carbon monoxide poisoning include headaches, dizziness, nausea, and drowsiness. A very small dosage of carbon monoxide can cause drowsiness, affecting perception (vision) and sapping driving alertness.

According to one expert, long before drivers lapse into unconsciousness, they may grow so drowsy that even if they see a curve or the road divider ahead, they may not have the strength, perception, or alertness to steer out of trouble.

Carbon monoxide–detecting chemical "pill."

➤ WHAT TO DO

1. While parked, if you feel the onset of a headache, dizziness, nausea, or loss of alertness, get out of the car and into fresh air. Shut off the engine and open the windows.
2. If you feel sleepy while driving, the cause may be carbon monoxide poisoning. Stop at once, get some fresh air, and breathe deeply to rid your system of possible carbon monoxide. Then drive with the windows open.
3. In slow-moving, closely spaced traffic, or while traveling in a confined area (like a highway tunnel), close all air vents or other air-intake systems to be sure that carbon monoxide from the exhausts of other cars will not infiltrate your car.
4. Periodically check, or have a mechanic inspect, your car for possible sources of carbon monoxide: leaking or defective engine gaskets, a loose or leaking engine manifold, a rusted or punctured tailpipe or muffler, any breaks in the connections of the exhaust system.
5. Even if you have never had a problem with carbon monoxide in your car, you might consider investing in a carbon monoxide detector. You can carry one on your person, clipped to a sun visor, or placed somewhere else inside the car. Available in some auto supply stores, the low-cost detector employs a small tablet containing a

sensitive chemical. The chemical, normally tan in color, turns progressively darker as the carbon monoxide level rises. If life-threatening levels of carbon monoxide are present, the chemical turns black in less than six minutes. Each detector tablet lasts about a month before needing replacement. These tablets, however, are not a substitute for getting your car fixed if there is a problem.

YOU SMELL GASOLINE

Unmistakably, and suddenly, you smell gasoline. Commuting the same route every day, you have now and again smelled faint whiffs of gasoline. But this time the smell is stronger, more pervasive. You can't shrug it off as "just a car smell."

➤ WHAT TO DO

1. If you're smoking, extinguish your cigarette. Get out of traffic immediately, park, and turn off the engine.
2. Inspect the car. Did you forget to replace the gas cap when you last refueled? If you discover that the cap is missing, you have probably found the source of the gasoline smell. Stuff a rag into the fuel fill pipe. Whatever you use to seal the pipe, it should be large and bulky enough not to slip into the gas tank.

   If the gas cap is securely in place, get down on all fours and inspect the gas tank for leaks. Gas tanks seldom leak unless they are old or have been punctured by something on the road. If you don't smell gasoline outside the car, turn to the engine compartment.
3. Raise the hood and search for any obvious leak in the fuel system or perhaps any gasoline leakage around the carburetor (if your car has one). Very little seepage can produce a strong odor of gasoline.

   Pinpointing the source of fuel leakage—any kind of leakage—in a crowded engine compartment can be difficult. But with persistence, and by investigating one section of the compartment at a time, fuel leaks can usually be uncovered, if they exist.
4. If you see nothing, and the gasoline smell seems to have disappeared, restart the engine with the hood still open. If you have a fire extinguisher, get it out and have it handy. Chances of a fire are small, but there is always that possibility with a gasoline leak.
5. With the engine running and fuel circulating, if you see a trickle of gasoline from a metal line (a fuel line), quickly shut down the engine. You've found the source of the gasoline smell. But can you somehow stop the leak long enough to drive safely to a repair shop?

If you suddenly smell gasoline, stop immediately and turn off the engine.

6. A repair is possible if you have a roll of duct tape and can reach the fuel line that needs repairing. Wrap the tape three or four times around the line and secure it in place. This should temporarily stop the leak.
7. Restart the engine. Inspect your repair. If you can't see or feel any wetness where the leak was, it is probably safe to drive to a repair shop.

Other fuel leaks may not be so easily stopped. Whether you can or even should attempt to repair them depends on your ability to make the repair, where the leak is located, and how large it is.

While the smell of gasoline can sometimes signal a driving emergency, some engine parts may leak gasoline without posing any immediate danger or even the threat of fire. As cars age, small fuel seepages are not unusual. These small leaks, especially in fuel system connections, can often be stopped with an application of duct tape or, if from a connection, by tightening the connection with an adjustable wrench.

Generally, a fuel leak that does not come in contact with the hot engine, or threaten to do so, is a leak you can drive a short distance with, if you cannot shut it off completely with an emergency repair.

PART 3

MECHANICAL EMERGENCIES

THE BRAKES SUDDENLY FAIL

In fast-moving traffic you ease on the brakes. Where you expected resistance—in the brake pedal—there is hardly any at all. As you push the pedal harder it sinks to the floorboard. Your brakes have suddenly failed.

➤ WHAT TO DO

1. "Pump" the brake pedal. Press it down, lift your foot, press it down again. Almost certainly, it will respond, as your pumping—much like priming a water pump—builds back some brake resistance, even though you may have lost much of your brakes' hydraulic fluid.
2. As the pedal responds, downshift into a lower "braking" gear. The combination of using a lower gear and pumping the brake pedal should slow the car.
3. Set the parking brake hard. The parking brake won't stop the car right away if you are traveling at traffic speed, but it will assist in braking the rear wheels.
4. Continue pumping the brake pedal. If it begins to fade again, pump it faster and harder. You should feel its resistance growing. Small as that resistance may be, it is acting to brake and slow you.

  Today's cars and trucks have a dual braking system, and sometimes a "split" braking system designed to prevent brake failure. It is improbable—and, in fact, all but impossible—for both or all of a modern vehicle's brakes to fail at the same time.

  What has probably happened is that a line carrying hydraulic braking fluid to one of the brakes has ruptured or the brake-fluid reservoir, the master cylinder, has lost much of its fluid due to leaking. By pumping the pedal, you prime the dual hydraulic system—maximizing any remaining hydraulic fluid. Thus, you usually have enough fluid and braking power to slow down, get to the shoulder or curb, and stop.

  Car owners can contribute to braking emergencies when they fail to heed a dashboard's brake system warning light and the warning chime that may accompany it, or neglect to have brakes checked regularly. Maintained brakes seldom fail.

  If brakes fail in rain, ice, or snow, the parking brake should not be used. Braking the rear wheels on slippery pavement may cause the car to skid, only compounding the emergency.

QUIET A DRAGGING MUFFLER OR TAILPIPE

If your car's tailpipe and muffler suddenly slip their brackets and begin dragging on the pavement, the sound isn't much different from the sound of tin cans being dragged behind a newlywed's car. Except the noise is louder because of the weight of the muffler and tailpipe.

➤ WHAT TO DO

1. Stop immediately. There's always the chance that the dragging tailpipe will become caught in your rear wheels or wedged beneath the chassis. If you have a car with rear-wheel drive, it can do serious damage to the drive shaft. Or it could break loose, causing drivers behind you to swerve to avoid your debris. Besides, you want to prevent further damage, if any, to the muffler and tailpipe. Once you find a garage or filling station, a mechanic may be able to reinstall both at modest cost. If you don't stop, passing motorists will probably make you embarrassingly aware of what you already know: your car is a rolling contributor to noise pollution.

2. All that's required is a quick fix: you need to secure the tailpipe and muffler so they won't drag. First, however, be sure the tailpipe assembly is cool. Then, using a length of twine, rope, even a straightened coat hanger or some easily tied wire, proceed with the repair.

   Wrap and tie one end of the rope or wire around the extreme end of the tailpipe (away from the hot parts). Thread the other end through, and over, any frame member or bracket. Lift the tailpipe and secure it by knotting (if you're using twine or rope) or by tying (wire) or bending (coat hanger). Be sure the tailpipe assembly is suspended far enough above the pavement to prevent further dragging.

   Securing the tailpipe assembly well above the pavement usually doesn't require your getting beneath the car. Kneeling, stooping, or sitting on the pavement should put you within easy reach of the tailpipe's end. In fact, some tailpipes conveniently protrude a few inches beyond the rear bumper, and within finger grasp. It is not only unnecessary to jack up the rear wheels to get at the tailpipe but also dangerous. Never work beneath a jacked-up car. Jacks can slip, pinning you beneath the car chassis.

3. With the tailpipe and muffler raised and secured to prevent drag, you're on your way to a mechanic. You've likely spent less than 10 minutes, start to finish. The work is usually that quick and easy.

THE RADIATOR TEMPERATURE WARNING COMES ON

If the dash's coolant temperature alert comes on it means that the radiator's coolant, and probably also the engine, are too hot. Do you face an immediate emergency? If you see steam coming from the hood, probably accompanied by hissing, it *is* an emergency. If you don't see steam or hear hissing from the hood, it has not yet become an emergency and may not.

A car can overheat for any number of nonemergency reasons:

- After a long drive at high speed, residual engine heat can cause the radiator's coolant temperature to rise high enough to trigger the coolant and engine alerts or to push the coolant gauge into the alert zone.
- Stop-and-go traffic idles your engine for long periods. Sustained idling, especially on hot days, has much the same coolant-heating effect as an engine shut down after a long, high-speed drive.
- If you tow something—a trailer, a boat, perhaps a second car—the load can make the engine work too hard. If it overheats, so will the radiator's coolant, which, piped through the engine, absorbs engine heat.
- Pulling a heavy load up a long, steep grade, especially in hot weather and at high altitudes, can also make the engine and its coolant overheat.

If an alert is accompanied by steam from under the hood, you face an emergency. An engine *that* hot can be ruined, its critical moving parts actually deformed, by extreme heat if you continue to drive. If the coolant is boiled out of the radiator, the engine can grow so hot that its fluids—oil and gasoline—may catch fire.

➤ WHAT TO DO

If the engine overheats but you see no steam:

1. If driving, slow down.
2. Turn off the air conditioner (it produces extra work for the engine).

3. Turn the heater on full blast (even if it's a hot day), and open the windows for your own comfort. The heater acts like an auxiliary radiator, helping to reduce coolant and engine temperature.
4. If you're in bumper-to-bumper traffic, shift as often as you can into neutral, which relieves the engine's workload.
5. If the coolant alert flicks off or the gauge's needle drops out of the warning zone, continue driving—but slowly.
6. Keep an eye on the instrument panel or gauge. If neither returns to alert status, you can drive normally.
7. If the panel or gauge warnings continue or return to alert status, still without steaming, pull to the shoulder and let the engine idle for a few minutes. Do not shut the engine off.
8. If the warnings stop, you can again drive at slow to moderate speeds.
9. Should the alert status continue, even with no steaming, pull off the road, park, and turn off the engine. You have no choice but to wait for the engine to cool.

If the engine overheats and steam rises from under the hood:

1. Immediately get to the road's shoulder and stop.
2. Shut off the engine.
3. You may want to have everyone get out of the car, particularly in an extreme engine-overheat situation. An engine that hot can (although few do) catch fire.
4. Do not raise the hood. There's no need for a visual check. You already know it's dangerously hot. There is a chance, again a small one, of engine fluids catching fire. Raising the hood when an engine is extremely hot will not appreciably cool it.
5. Wait out the cooling period (until the engine and the radiator no longer steam). When steaming ceases, raise the hood. At this point, raising it—particularly if there's a breeze or the roadside temperature is cool—may help speed engine cooling.

COOL AN OVERHEATED ENGINE AND RADIATOR

Something hisses and steams under the hood. Almost immediately—but likely moments before—the instrument panel's hot engine alert flashes on or the needle on the coolant temperature gauge climbs into the warning zone.

Your car's radiator and the engine are overheating, perhaps dangerously so.

➤ WHAT TO DO

1. Pull off the road immediately and stop. Before you turn off the engine, try this: set the parking brake, put the transmission in Neutral and run the engine at fast idle for a minute or two. You may notice a drop in engine gauge temperature or the warning light may flick off. (Despite this, the coolant and engine may still be extremely hot.) Then put the car in Park or in gear, and shut off the engine. The hissing and steaming may reoccur or increase due to a buildup of residual engine heat.

2. Wait until the engine cools enough to safely open the hood. Opening it while the radiator is boiling risks a bad burn or scalding, and will not significantly hurry the engine's cooling. Even the metal you must grasp to open the hood may be too hot to handle.

3. When the hissing and steaming have stopped (wait at least 10 minutes), lift the hood. Before you do anything else, look for obvious leaks or breaks in the radiator's hoses, in the radiator itself, or around the clamps that may fix the hoses to the upper and lower outlet and inlet pipes of the radiator.

   If the radiator fan is driven by a belt, check to make sure the belt isn't broken or loose. Be supercautious and keep your hands and clothing away from the fan if it is electrically powered. Belt-driven fans stop when the engine stops. Electrically driven belts can start up at anytime, whether the engine is on or off.

4. When the radiator is cooler, test the coolant system's pressure before attempting to remove the radiator's cap. To test the pressure, squeeze the top radiator hose. If it's soft and only slightly warm to the touch, the radiator is no longer highly pressurized.

Some highway departments cache water at points along steep grades where cars overheat.

That does not mean, however, that no pressure exists. (To relieve pressure in some cars, you can flip a pressure-release lever.)

5. Prepare to remove the radiator cap. Put rags over the cap to prevent getting burned by the hot radiator. Through the cloth, grasp the cap and turn it a fraction of an inch. If there is any hissing, stop. Do not attempt to remove the cap. Hissing indicates that the system is still under considerable pressure, perhaps enough pressure to cause hot coolant to erupt if you open the cap.

6. Wait another 10 minutes or so, then try again. Still using rags to shield your hands and face, test the cap as before. If there is no hissing, remove the cap.

7. Assuming you can find a gallon or two of water, add it to the coolant-recovery tank

that's linked to the radiator by a thin tube. Before adding water, note the level of coolant in the recovery tank. Marks at various levels on most recovery tanks indicate how much coolant remains in the system. The water you add will supplement whatever coolant remains but is only a stopgap measure until you reach a service shop for a revitalization of the coolant mix.

8. Loosely replace the radiator cap. Do not tighten it. Leaving the cap loose ensures that little if any pressure will rebuild in the system. You don't want to revive the pressure to the previous level. You can, in fact, leave the cap off or hold it loosely in place with a piece of duct tape.

9. With the engine cooled, water added, and cap loosely replaced, you should be able to drive at reduced speed to the nearest service station.

PATCH A LEAKY RADIATOR HOSE

From the driver's seat, the first sign of trouble is as close as your car's hood: a few wisps of steam. Perhaps, too, radiator coolant begins percolating from the edges of the hood, where hood and body meet. If your car has a coolant temperature gauge, its needle may be positioned slightly higher than normal. As for today's more common coolant digital readout or lighted panel alerts, it takes time for the coolant temperature to grow hot enough to activate them.

You don't, however, need gauges or dash-panel warnings to tell you that something is wrong. The evidence—those wisps of steam and water bubbling from the hood—is obvious. Even if you're not a car buff, you can probably guess what's wrong: either the radiator or one of its hoses has sprung a leak.

Pull off the road, set the parking brake, put the transmission in Park (for an automatic) or in Neutral (for a manual), leave the engine idling (an idling engine maintains coolant system pressure and will make a leak more obvious), and carefully lift the hood. Hot coolant may be spurting from the radiator's top hose—the hose through which hot coolant returns from the engine to the radiator for cooling. Less obvious leaks include a leak in the radiator's bottom hose, which is usually harder to reach and inspect and is too often neglected during routine checkups; a leak around the clamps that hold the radiator's two hoses—top and bottom—to the radiator's inlet and outlet pipes; and a leak in the radiator itself. Wherever the leak is, you need to stop it, or at least diminish it, so as not to lose so much coolant that the radiator boils before you can reach a service station for a permanent fix.

➤ WHAT TO DO

1. Carefully observe what's leaking and precisely where it's leaking.
2. If you can, mark the spot (without being burned by the hot coolant). When you shut off the engine the leak may disappear as coolant system pressure subsides.
3. Shut off the engine and let things cool. You may have to wait 10 to 20 minutes before the radiator is cool enough to risk loosening and removing the radiator's cap.
4. When the radiator is reasonably cool, place several layers of rags over the cap and loosen the cap slightly to let steam and pressure escape into the rag. Then carefully remove the cap.

147

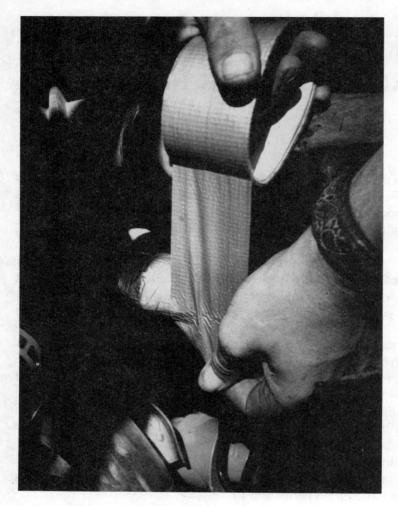

**Wrap duct tape around
the radiator hose.**

5. Patching a leak in a radiator hose is relatively easy. Almost any stout adhesive wrapping will stop, or significantly reduce, a leak. In an emergency, use whatever you have at hand: a first-aid kit's adhesive tape, tire tape (a black, sticky, clothlike tape), or, better, duct tape. Some people have even used masking tape or plastic wrap. Such unlikely leak-stoppers can often work if you replace the radiator cap loosely so that only a little pressure builds in the system when you start the car.

6. Wrap the hose tightly. Apply five or six layers around the leaky spot.

7. Even leaks in the radiator can be reduced, if not completely stopped, with patches of duct tape, especially a leak at the top of the radiator where tape can fit over the radiator's honeycomb core.

8. If the leak is around a radiator hose clamp, first tighten the clamp with a screw-

driver. Most hose clamps are the ratchet type, tightened with a screw. Wrap the clamp and adjacent hose with tape.

9. Replace the radiator cap, but don't tighten it. Leave it loose. The loose cap will prevent pressure buildup in the coolant system. With pressure reduced, almost any makeshift hose, clamp, or radiator patch will probably hold until a mechanic can make repairs.

10. In hot or cold weather, turn the heater on full blast. Radiator water circulating through the heater will help keep coolant temperature down.

THE BATTERY ISN'T CHARGING

While driving, the dashboard's battery charging light ("idiot" light) goes on. Or, if your car has gauges, you notice that the "charge" indicator is pointing to the zero mark, or somewhere in the gauge's negative—discharging—zone.

Whether indicated by a warning light or gauge, one thing is certain (discounting the possibility of a faulty warning or an electrical short circuit): the car's battery is no longer being charged by the alternator or generator. Worse, depending on what electricity-using accessories are being used—headlights, air conditioner, heater, radio, stereo, and the like—the battery is discharging. And, if you're driving after dark with the headlights on, it may be happening rapidly. Headlights generally use more of the battery's energy than any other single power-using accessory, other than the momentary huge power demand of the starter motor when you start the engine.

Provided you immediately heed the dashboard's "no charge" or "discharge" warning, your battery is in good condition, and you take steps to minimize the amount of current drawn from the battery's ever-dwindling reservoir of electricity, there's no need to panic. If a battery is fully or nearly fully charged when the "no charge" or "discharge" signal comes on, it will still provide up to 20 to 25 minutes of power. That is usually enough power to operate the power-using accessories necessary to get you to a garage or mechanic.

➤ WHAT TO DO

1. Pull to the shoulder or curb when you safely can.
2. Don't turn off the engine. Leave the engine running in Neutral or Park to avoid a potential battery-draining restart attempt. Methodically turn off *every* power-using accessory. (At night, your hazard lights will have to be left on.) If the dashboard is lighted, dim or turn off even its minimal electric lights.
3. Once you've reduced power needs, sit back for a moment and plan your next move. Should you get out, lift the hood, and attempt to find the problem, assuming it's as obvious as a busted alternator or generator belt or an equally obvious worn and shorted battery cable? The decision is yours. Car buffs would probably opt to look under the hood. Minor battery or cable problems can generally be quickly corrected: corroded battery clamps can be brushed clean or, if loose, tightened with an adjust-

150

able wrench. An obvious worn spot in the battery cables' insulation can often be quickly remedied by wrapping the exposed area with a strip of rag or with duct tape.

But most drivers, with no particular mechanical bent or curiosity, will probably—and perhaps wisely—decide merely to get off the road and to a mechanic as soon as possible. Although the battery isn't being recharged, it may still have enough energy to fire the spark plugs, thus keeping the engine running. The plain fact is there isn't, normally, much you can do roadside to quick-fix a no-charge battery problem. The savviest strategy is to resume driving to the nearest garage or filling station, while nursing—using as few battery-energized devices as possible—your ebbing power reserve.

CHANGE A BATTERY

Knowing how to change a battery—and change it correctly—can extricate you from situations like the following:

Your battery dies late at night, perhaps in your own driveway or miles from home. You find a filling station that will sell you a replacement, but the station attendant tells you the mechanic will not be available until morning. You can install it yourself or wait until the mechanic shows up for work.

Or, at a winter resort, you attempt to start your car after leaving it out all night in the cold, but the car won't start, and you have an appointment four hours away back at the office. The resort will loan you a battery, but you will have to install it.

Or, your car battery, which has already received one recent boost, shows sudden signs of continued weakness. You have a dozen appointments and simply don't trust the battery to get you where you're going and home again. Until you find time to have a new battery installed, you have to borrow the battery from your wife's car.

Changing a battery isn't difficult if you don't mind a bit of dirt and grime.

➤ WHAT TO DO

1. With a wrench, disconnect the battery's *negative* cable, which is clamped to the battery's *negative* terminal post. The negative post is identified by a minus symbol ($-$) or the abbreviation NEG. If the battery also has a *negative* ground wire (a few batteries do), disconnect it using a screwdriver or a wrench. A ground wire is usually attached to the engine. Finally, disconnect the *positive* cable from the *positive* battery post. It's labeled with a plus sign ($+$) or the abbreviation POS.

2. Removing the battery cable clamps can be difficult when a battery is old and its terminal posts and clamps are corroded or bonded by rust to one another. To remove a clamp, first loosen its bolt and nut. They hold and squeeze the clamp in close electrical contact with its post.

    Whereas some batteries dispense with bolt and clamp post-fasteners, the majority (probably) still use them. The bolt usually has two square-headed nuts. One is part of the bolt (stationary); the other is threaded to the bolt. Often you need two holding tools—an adjustable wrench and a vise-type grip pliers—to remove them.

With both negative and positive cables disconnected, lift the battery free.

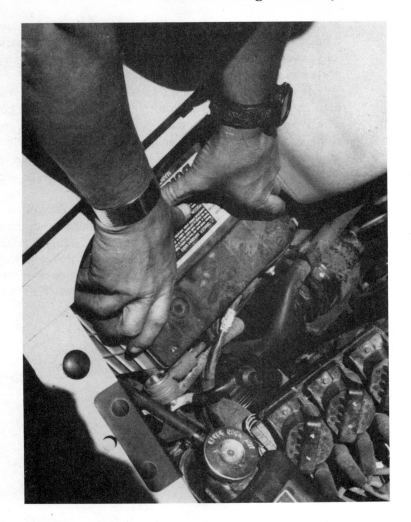

Lock the bolt head with pliers and use the wrench to loosen and unscrew the threaded bolt. Or switch tool positions, if that's easier and gives you a better grip.

Even with the bolt and its nut loosened, you may have to pry the clamp from the terminal post. In prying, you *don't* want to put any pressure on the battery terminal itself. Doing so can easily crack the battery case or punch a hole right through it.

To pry the clamps from their posts, use a screwdriver to force apart the clamp's jaws. As you pry open the jaws, work the clamp back and forth on its post, loosening the bond between them. If a clamp won't slip upward and off its post, squirt the post and clamp with a lubricant.

With the cables and their clamps freed from the posts, remove the battery and put it aside.

3. Set the replacement battery in position (on the tray where the old battery was) and lubricate its posts. You can use any handy lubricant, including grease, petroleum jelly, even motor oil. A lubricant eases the clamps more easily over their battery posts and postpones corrosion.

If you're installing an old or used battery, before reinstalling the clamps, and before applying a lubricant, clean each post to remove corrosion or rust. Any handy abrasive will scour them clean, enhancing electrical contact with the clamps. A slurry of baking soda and water usually does the job. So will sandpaper. Even a little sand mixed with radiator water—both readily available wherever the emergency occurs—are credible battery terminal cleaners. With the old posts clean, lubricate them before reinstalling their clamps.

If you're installing a new battery, its terminal posts should already be clean and corrosion-free. It will need no special attention other than application of a lubricant.

4. Now slip the *positive* cable clamp over the battery's *positive* terminal post and install the *negative* clamp and its negative cable on the *negative* post. If the battery also has a negative ground cable, reattach it to the engine or wherever it was connected.

5. Finally, retighten the clamp bolts and their nuts. They've got to be as tight as possible to ensure good electrical contact.

JUMP-START YOUR CAR

"**B**ooster cables" are handy emergency electrical cables—the "positive" cable is usually colored red, the "negative" cable is usually black, both with "alligator" clamps at each end—that can get a car with a weak or nearly dead battery going when nothing else can. However, they must be used properly to work safely.

At one time or another, you have probably used booster cables to jump-start your car. For example, you may have stopped at a restaurant and left the headlights on. When you returned to your car, it wouldn't start. The headlights had drained the battery of the power it needed to turn the starter motor fast enough to start the engine.

Or, on a hot day in bumper-to-bumper traffic, you may have whiled away the tedium with the radio and air conditioner going full blast. When you got home and parked, you had no reason to suspect there was a problem. But in the morning, when you tried to start the car, it was unresponsive. A combination of small problems—perhaps a slipping alternator belt or an already weak battery, and that stop-and-go commute that never permitted the battery to fully recharge—created an emergency (the car won't start and you need to get to work on time).

Or, on a cold winter morning, you may have switched on the ignition and heard an anemic, half-hearted attempt by the starter motor to crank the engine. The cold had sapped the battery of its starting power.

Common emergencies such as these call for a boost—a quick jolt of auxiliary power to get the engine started. Once it's started and you're on your way, the alternator or generator will recharge the battery (assuming it's in good condition).

If you are a member of an auto club, and you face a battery emergency within its service area, you can phone for emergency service. (Some car manufacturers also provide similar road service.) Tow trucks are equipped to boost batteries. Or you can haul your own booster cables from the trunk and have someone give you a boost.

➤ WHAT TO DO

1. There's a right way and a dangerously wrong way to jump-start a battery. Do it incorrectly, and you can ruin your battery. You can also cause it to catch fire, even to explode with the force of a small bomb.

   To do it safely, the booster cables must be correctly attached. Just as important

Booster cables from the booster car are run to the car being boosted.

is the order in which the boosting battery's negative and positive terminal posts are attached to the negative and positive terminal posts of your battery.

Batteries are potentially dangerous to work around, although the newer no-maintenance types are sealed, eliminating some of the danger. Batteries produce highly volatile and explosive hydrogen gas. They are also the source of skin- and eye-burning sulfuric acid. And even a weak battery can be discharged (if you accidentally short its two terminals) with enough electrical energy to give you a jolt. Fully-charged batteries pack enough electricity to severely injure.

When boosting your battery, use simple precautions. Don't smoke or light up near the battery. Boost, if you can, in an open area rather than in an enclosed place, such as a garage. Remove any metal jewelry or other metal objects that might brush the battery's terminals and cause the battery to short and discharge. If you are using any metal tools, work on only one terminal—whether the negative or positive—at a time to avoid shorting the battery and risking an electric shock. Never permit the boosting vehicle to come in contact with your own. Although your car and the booster's car may be positioned bumper-to-bumper, particularly if booster cables are short, absolutely do not let the bumpers touch.

2. Inspect the terminal posts and the cable clamps (which are fastened to the posts) for corrosion. Excessive corrosion acts as an insulator, impeding the flow of current from one battery to the other.

   Remove as much corrosion as you can. Mechanics use a small scrub brush and a mixture of water (about a quart) and baking soda or ammonia (a cup of either mixed with the water). Since it's unlikely you'll have either ammonia or baking soda on hand, use anything abrasive to rid battery posts and their clamps of corrosion, for example, sandpaper, even sand mixed with water (from the radiator) can be applied with a toothbrush or with a handy rag. Clean one terminal at a time.

   Also, inspect the battery post clamps. They should be tightly connected. If not, tighten the clamp with an adjustable wrench or vise-grip pliers.

3. Have the booster position his or her car so that the booster cables, which vary in length, reach from one battery to the other. Usually this means that cars must be positioned with their "battery side" closest together. That, or positioned front bumper to front bumper.

4. Turn off both cars' ignitions, lights, radios—anything that uses battery power.

5. Now follow this procedure—*exactly:*

   Clamp one of the red (positive) cable clamps to the *positive* terminal of the *booster car's* battery.

   Clamp the *same* cable's opposite end to the *positive* terminal of *your* battery. (A plus sign [+] or the abbreviation POS near the terminal will identify the positive posts.)

   Clamp one of the black (negative) cable clamps to the *booster battery's negative* terminal post. The negative has a minus sign (−) or the abbreviation NEG near it.

   Clamp the *same* cable's opposite end to a piece of unpainted metal, like a part of the car (not the grill or the radiator).

6. With booster cables in place, get into your car. Put the key in the ignition and shift into Neutral or Park. Then, when you're behind the wheel and ready, signal the other driver. He or she will start the other car's engine and accelerate to modest speed. As the engine revs up, turn the key in your ignition. The boost your battery will get from the other battery should crank and start your engine.

7. Let both engines idle as you remove the booster cables. Follow this removal procedure—*exactly:*

   First, remove the *negative* clamp from the metal you clamped it to.

Next, remove the *negative* clamp from the *booster's* battery.

Then, remove the *positive* clamp from *your* battery.

Finally, remove the *positive* clamp from the *booster's* battery.

(When you are hooking or unhooking a clamp, be careful not to let its opposite clamp touch anything metal on the car.)

8. With your engine started, drive for at least 20 minutes (on a highway, if possible) to give the alternator or generator a chance to recharge your battery. A little speed recharges your battery quicker. Avoid street traffic. At a stoplight or in stop-and-go traffic, the engine might die before your battery has the power to restart it.

RELEASE A STUCK SEAT BELT

$\mathbf{S}$eat belts are lifesavers. But they can also kill if you can't get unbuckled when your life depends on it: the car rolls over, catches fire, plunges into a lake, is involved in a flaming multicar pileup, or is engulfed by a sudden flash flood. If a buckle fails you at a stoplight as an attacker jumps in through an unlocked door, you may not be able to escape. There are times when you simply need to unbuckle quickly.

➤ WHAT TO DO

If your shoulder and lap belt have no emergency release:

1. Pull as hard as you can on the webbing as you depress the buckle's release button (or, in old-style belts, flip up the buckle's hinged top).
2. If the tongue still won't release (the fault may be yours for not lubricating the belt mechanism, or for allowing it to collect grime and dirt), try springing the belt's locking mechanism.

   Depending on the type of buckle your seat belts have, you can sometimes insert a nail file, one prong of a tweezers, a screwdriver (if you keep one in the glove compartment), or anything similar into the side of the buckle or into its tongue entrance way, and depress or raise the mechanism holding the tongue.
3. That failing, go for the jugular: cut through the belt's webbing to free yourself. Any glass shard, used carefully so as not to cut your fingers, can be used as a saw. Smash a mirror (for example, the visor's mirror) against the dash. Or, with the heel of your shoe, break the driver-side mirror. If you wear eyeglasses with glass lenses, in an emergency you may have to sacrifice one of them to cut yourself free. Twist the eyeglass frame and the lenses will pop out. With fingers gripping opposite sides of a lens, break it over anything in the driver's compartment. You have quickly devised an effective cutting tool.
4. Wrap your hand in something protective. Grip the glass shard firmly and begin sawing across the belt's width.
5. To speed the cutting process, try weakening the web by burning a path where you

159

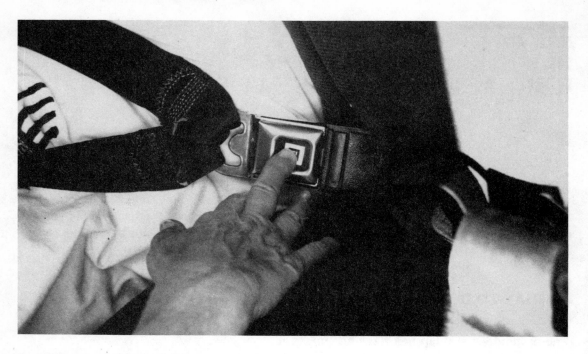

Releasing a stuck seat belt.

> intend to cut. As burning tools you can use a cigarette lighter (not the car's electrical one, which singes rather than burns and doesn't remain hot for very long, but the flame type) or a match. It'll require a number of matches to burn a path through the webbing.
>
> 6. With a sharp shard of glass and a fire-weakened belt, cutting can be done surprisingly fast—hopefully, fast enough to extricate you from your emergency.

If your shoulder or lap belt has an emergency release:

1. Some cars also provide an emergency release mechanism for shoulder harness and lap belt combinations. Some provide it only for the shoulder harness.
2. To release your shoulder belt, reach above and behind you (the emergency release is located near the shoulder belt's retractor and is almost identical in appearance to a lap belt buckle, except that it may be labeled PRESS IN EMERGENCY).
3. Press the release button, and the shoulder harness is freed from its restraint. In some cases you'll still have to cut through the lap-belt webbing to release that part of the safety harness.

CHECK AND REPLACE FUSES

You turn the key in the ignition and nothing happens. It could be a problem with the fuse powering the ignition. Both headlights suddenly fail. The fault is more likely a fuse or circuit breaker than the headlight bulbs. You're driving through a blizzard when the wipers stop dead and stay dead. Snow overload may have worked the wipers too hard, causing the fuse that energizes them to blow. When you need them most, the hazard flashers and brake lights don't work. Look to a fuse or circuit breaker as the possible cause of your emergency signal blackout.

In an emergency, you may have to replace or exchange fuses. Yet most drivers don't know where their car's fuse box is, let alone how to change fuses or manipulate circuit breakers. And many late model cars have a fuse box inside the car and another under the hood.

When replacing or checking fuses or breakers, consult your owner's manual.

To prepare yourself for this kind of driving emergency, or simply to learn more about your car, you can turn to your owner's manual. The location and content of fuse boxes vary from car to car, even model to model. Your owner's manual will tell you where your car's fuse box or boxes are; the electrical rating (amperage) of each fuse, breaker, or fuse link (another kind of fuse); and what electrical accessories or circuits each controls.

Typically, a fuse box may be mounted underneath or in the glove compartment, on the steering column, or under the dashboard near the parking brake release. Some fuse boxes contain extra fuses of various power ratings, plus a handy little tool (a fuse puller) for removing fuses. Car electrical breakers work just like your breakers at home: push them one direction and they shut off electricity to the circuits they control, push them the opposite way and they reenergize the circuits. Many fuse boxes list the fuses and breakers they contain, what each does, and their electrical ratings.

If you replace a fuse, make sure the replacement has the same, or a *lower*, power rating. The reason is simple: a fuse's job is to protect an often delicate electrical circuit from electrical overload. If a five-ampere fuse burns out (and shuts off electricity to whatever system or instruments it protects) and you replace it with one of twice the rating, you've put the circuits controlled by that fuse at risk. That's probably more current than the circuit and its instruments can withstand (an expensive gauge or other component can be destroyed).

To replace a fuse, for example if your horn is defective and won't stop blasting, follow these steps.

➤ WHAT TO DO

1. Open the fuse box's lid to expose its fuses, breakers, and fuse links.
2. From your owner's manual list and explanations of fuses and breakers, or from the fuse box's own listing, determine which fuse controls the horn and the fuse's power (amperage) rating.
3. You may find that the horn's fuse also powers the cigarette lighter. If you remove the fuse, silencing the horn, you will also deactivate the cigarette lighter.
4. If you decide you can do without the cigarette lighter, remove the fuse by using the fuse puller that's in the fuse box or virtually anything else (a pencil will do) that can pry the fuse from its holder. As the fuse comes out, the horn should go silent.
5. If you want to fix a horn that doesn't work, you need to know if the problem is with the horn's fuse or the horn itself. Run a quick test to find out. If the cigarette lighter and the other items run by the same fuse are working, it can't be the fuse. The problem is the horn or its wiring.
6. If your quick test shows that none of the items on the horn's circuit are working, remove the horn's fuse and inspect it. If the metal strip inside the fuse is burned through, or the fuse's interior looks milky, the fuse is blown.
7. Before replacing it, turn off the car's ignition. Then replace the blown fuse with a

spare (often in the fuse box) of the same electrical rating or lower. If there is no spare fuse, you may be able to borrow one with the same or lower rating from another of the car's circuits, provided the accessories powered by that fuse aren't critical to your immediate driving emergency.

If an accessory has blown its fuse, there may be a short or other trouble in the accessory. Have your dealer or mechanic check to see what, if anything, is wrong.

GET YOUR CAR GOING
IF IT RUNS OUT OF GAS

With the gas gauge or digital fuel indicator showing all but empty, you gambled—and lost. The engine sputters, chokes, and quits. You're out of gas. Assuming you somehow got out of traffic, and managed to reach the highway's shoulder or the curb, what do you do?

If you're traveling on a highway during daylight, you may be able to get help from a passing motorist. Provided you find a willing donor and a siphoning kit, you may be able to siphon a few gallons of gas from that driver's tank, enough to get you to the nearest filling station.

Or, if you're in town, you can walk to a gas station, but unless your gas container has a funnellike spigot, you won't be able to pour the gasoline from the can into your car's tank (most of it will end up on the pavement). However, you can quickly craft a funnel from newspapers, a magazine, or almost anything else you can roll up.

➤ WHAT TO DO

If you run out of gas at night on a freeway:

Raise the hood, set up light reflectors (if you have them), and lock yourself in the car until a police car arrives. Ask the police to phone for road service. A tow truck driver can give you gasoline or tow you (for a fee, of course) to the nearest open gas station.

If you run out of gas at night in town:

1. If a gas station is nearby, and you know the area, decide whether it's safe to walk the short distance to the station.
2. If the walk may be unsafe, phone for help from the nearest public or business phone (at an all-night restaurant, for instance). Phone your auto club, a friend, your spouse, your parents, or, if necessary, the police. Inform them of your plight. Whomever you call can stop at a filling station and bring you a gallon or two of gas.

164

If you run out of gas on a freeway, raise the hood and wait for police or a tow truck.

3. In a suspect part of town, hail a cab (even for a short drive) to transport you to and from the nearest gas station.

If you run out of gas on a distant, lonely road:

1. The "farm to market" roads, which bind rural America to towns and cities, are driven by a high proportion of local—and often helpful—people. Where you would hesitate to accept a ride from a stranger to the nearest gas station in the city, in rural America, it is often less dangerous. And once you reach a local service station, you can almost always get a ride back to your car, tote can in hand.
2. If you can't get a ride into town, someone may offer you a few gallons of gas from his or her car tank, so be prepared to use your siphoning kit to extract it.

QUICK-FIX
A POWER-STEERING HOSE LEAK

It may begin with a smell—the unmistakable smell of oil burning under the hood. Perhaps, at the same time, steering seems more difficult. You may also hear the faint beginnings of a grinding sound. Your car's power steering system is failing fast, if it has not already failed altogether.

After parking, leave the engine running and lift the hood. You may be shocked at what you see: a reddish fluid—power-steering fluid—may be spurting from somewhere. The oily stuff has splattered over the engine, disfigured engine accessories, and stained the sound-deadening material on the hood's underside. The hose of your power-steering system has sprung a leak. That's not unusual, considering the power-steering system's hose carries pressure greater than any hose in most cars.

When faced with a power-steering hose leak, you can still drive the car—although without power steering—to the nearest repair shop, whether the hose break occurs in town or on the highway, provided you have stopped the leak from the power-steering hose (see What to Do if the Power Steering Suddenly Fails, page 222).

But you shouldn't drive the car as long as the power-steering hose is spurting or gushing steering fluid because the fluid, although not nearly as volatile as gasoline, can nonetheless be ignited by the hot engine—in particular, by the engine's manifold, where hot exhaust gases exit the engine. Driving the car in that condition risks fire under the hood. In addition, your power-steering unit may be ruined if the leak has depleted the steering fluid, because the power-steering pump uses the fluid as a lubricant.

➤ WHAT TO DO

1. Shut off the engine. That will temporarily stop the leak.
2. You've got to stop the outpouring of steering fluid, which will resume once you start the engine again. You can attempt to repair the leak (easy in some situations, and for some makes and models), or, if too much fluid has already leaked out, you can cut the engine belt that drives the power-steering pump. You'll ruin the belt, of course, and need to have a new one installed, but you'll save the pump and steering unit,

which can cost many times more than the price of a new belt. With the leak stopped, and the power-steering pump literally put out of action—when you cut the belt powering it—you can safely drive to the nearest repair shop or filling station.

But if your car has a serpentine belt—powering not just the steering unit pump but probably also the alternator, the air-conditioning compressor, and other accessories—the easy fix becomes more difficult. The radiator fan, likely electric-powered, not belt-powered, can still work even if you cut the serpentine belt. In addition, you can do without battery charging and air-conditioning for the short drive to a repair shop. But before you cut it, be very sure that the radiator fan is powered separately, and not powered by the serpentine belt. You can do without most belt-driven accessories, but not for very long without an operating radiator fan.

3. Stop the leak. Because the spurting fluid is under extremely high pressure, most tapes—like masking, "tire," or electrical tape—won't hold the leak, or hold it for very long. What's required—and what usually will temporarily shut off the flow—is tougher tape: a cloth-backed tape, such as duct tape or heavy "pipe wrap," a rubberlike, plastic-backed tape used by plumbers to stop pipe leaks, including high pressure leaks. Wrap the power-steering hose at the rupture site with either of these heftier tapes and chances are you'll stop the leak.

Even so, in many engine compartments of newer model cars you face the problem of reaching the power-steering hose and finding enough room to wrap it. Today's engine compartments are so crammed with accessories that everything is harder to reach and fix. Power-steering hoses are no exception.

Still, assuming you have the stouter tape and have room enough to wrap the hose's leak area, the wrapping is easy. Hold the end of the tape roll in one hand. Firm the end over the leak area with thumb and forefinger and begin wrapping. Six to eight layers of wrap should be sufficient to seal off the leak.

Start the engine, and examine the hose to make sure the leak has stopped. Also, listen for any grinding sounds coming from the power-steering pump. If you hear grinding, immediately shut off the engine. Although you've stopped the hose leak, so much power-steering fluid has likely leaked out that the power-steering pump is running "dry." Without something to lubricate it, the pump will shortly tear itself to pieces.

You have at least one quick-fix solution other than cutting the pump's drivebelt: simply use regular motor oil to lubricate the power-steering pump. It is preferable to use power-steering fluid, but regular motor oil—assuming you have a can of it in the car or can borrow one from another motorist—will do in an emergency. Motor oil won't damage the pump. Besides, any filling station can replace the motor oil with steering fluid. Simply remove the power-steering reservoir cap and pour the motor oil into the uncapped fill pipe. This will temporarily solve the problem of a dry pump.

Your other option is to cut the single drivebelt, or the multidrive serpentine belt, that drives the power-steering pump.

4. Cut the power-steering belt. Use a pocket knife or anything else capable of cutting. You don't have to be a mechanic or know much about what's under the hood to find the belt that powers the steering pump. Locate the power-steering pump unit. It is the only belt-driven unit (a capped reservoir) with a fill pipe for adding fluid. The belt driving it is the one to cut, whether it's a single belt or a multidrive serpentine belt. Then cut the belt and remove it from the pulleys it runs on. (Removing a serpentine belt from its pulleys is not easy. You may have to use a screwdriver to pry the belt off its pulleys and from around the knoblike tensioner that's part of the serpentine drive.)

Cut the belt and you stop the pump—the pump stops turning (thus can't damage itself), and there's no longer any pressure in the power-steering system. This may save the power-steering unit from self-destructing. However, if you cut a serpentine belt, you'll be without battery charging and air-conditioning until you can find a repair shop.

With the power-steering belt cut, you can drive to a repair shop without damage to the power-steering system or its pump. Driving may be difficult, but with both hands on the steering wheel, and a bit of effort, you can drive out of trouble.

A WIPER BLADE BREAKS ON THE ROAD

While driving through heavy rain or snow, with your wipers on a high setting, the driver-side wiper suddenly breaks. Either the rubber squeegee works loose, disappears, or the entire wiper assembly breaks.

Wiper failure is rare, but it happens. When it does, it's usually because few drivers regularly check their wipers. Most experts say that wiper blades (the rubber squeegee) should be replaced at least every 12 months, and more frequently—every six months—if you frequently drive in rain or snow.

To restore the driver-side wiper, and possibly save the windshield from scratches made by the bladeless wiper arm, you will have to take some action.

➤ WHAT TO DO

1. Turn off the wipers. Slowly signal your intent to make for the road's shoulder and, once safely out of traffic, stop and size up your situation. One thing is certain: you can't drive through the rain or snow without driver-side visibility.

   If you are familiar with the area you're driving through, and you can be pretty sure the storm will abate within a reasonable time, the solution is simple. Wait out the storm. When the worst of it is over, affording enough visibility to drive without a wiper, you can drive to the nearest filling station for a blade or even a wiper assembly replacement.

2. If, however, you believe there will be no early abatement of rain or snow, and you need or want to get going, you'll have to borrow the squeegee blade from the passenger-side wiper, or even the whole wiper assembly, and install it on the driver side.

   If you choose to do this, consider a few things. First, while removing the squeegee from one wiper blade and installing it in the other is usually a simple process on most cars, there are exceptions. Removal and reinstallation of the entire wiper assembly may be more difficult, depending on the make and model of your car. If you're in the habit of changing blades or the whole assembly, you already know how to do it. Generally, no tools are required.

   But having borrowed the passenger-side blade, you face another problem: how

169

If your driver-side wiper blade breaks, you can borrow the passenger-side blade.

do you prevent the bladeless wiper arm from scratching the passenger-side windshield? One solution is to borrow the entire wiper assembly. If you decide to borrow just the passenger-side blade, you'll have to do something to prevent the arm from scratching the windshield.

Wrapping the bladeless wiper arm in duct tape may solve this problem. Then, again, you may have no choice but to bend the bladeless arm so that it does not contact the windshield. The risk in distorting the arm is that you'll have to replace the entire wiper unit. In a car emergency, doing some damage to achieve a quick fix is not uncommon. Even so, the cost of replacing the passenger-side wiper unit is small compared with the cost of replacing a scratched windshield.

Most blade assemblies are removed this way: you squeeze a clasp that releases the blade assembly from the wiper arm. When you insert the "borrowed" blade assembly from the passenger-side wiper unit into the driver-side wiper unit, the clasps close to lock the blade assembly onto the wiper arm.

3. With the borrowed blade or blade assembly transferred to the driver-side wiper unit, turn on the windshield's washer (if your car is equipped with one) to lubricate the windshield while you test the transferred wiper blade's performance.

If the blade isn't making contact over its entire rubber surface with the windshield's glass, bend the wiper arm slightly until it does. When the wiper arm is exactly parallel to the windshield, the blade should be in full contact with the glass. To bend the wiper arm, use pliers (vise-grip pliers are best).

But you can do the bending without tools. Hold the wiper arm with two hands, one hand near the arm's tip, the other near its base. Bend gently. You may have to bend several times before the wiper arm, held parallel with the windshield, achieves uniform rubber-to-glass contact.

THE HEADLIGHTS SUDDENLY FAIL

Few driving emergencies are more frightening than a headlight outage. On a less traveled highway (especially if you're speeding), particularly a rural road, sudden headlight failure can be terrifying. One moment your lights bathe the road ahead, the next you are driving blind in total darkness. How do you steer for the shoulder when you don't even know where the shoulder is?

On a trafficked highway, with cars ahead and behind you, you can see and react to their lights. Oncoming traffic can also offer some road illumination, as can light posts along the road. You may be without headlights, but you are not totally in the dark.

➤ WHAT TO DO

1. For the moment, maintain your speed.
2. Quickly check to see if only your high or low beams are out. You may, in fact, have one or the other still working. If you have neither, check to see if you have lost total power.

    If you have a system failure, the engine will quit, its spark plugs no longer energized (see What to Do in a Total Electrical Failure on page 224).
3. If the engine is still operating, indicating a specific, nonsystem failure, quickly test all your lights: the turn indicators, the interior light, even the fog lights or other specialty lights, like off-road lights or spotlights.
4. If all the lights except your headlights are working, getting out of traffic and to the highway's shoulder or right lane should not be difficult. Switch on your four-way hazard lights to alert traffic that you have a problem.
5. Prepare to change lanes by making certain there's no oncoming traffic to your right. Indicate your intention with the turn signal, and get into the right lane or onto the shoulder. (For your turn signal to work, you may have to switch off your hazard lights because they often don't operate simultaneously.)
6. Leave the highway at the next exit. On lighted city streets you should be able to find a service station or reach home, even without headlights. In the morning a mechanic can correct the problem.

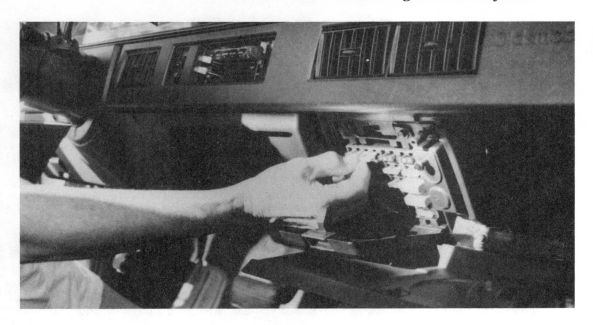

To find out which fuse or breaker powers the headlights, consult your owner's manual.

THE ENGINE BLOWS A GASKET

Y̲ou're driving around town or on the highway when your car begins to sound like a truck. Under the hood something is making a deafening noise. Your engine has blown a gasket.

On the highway, perhaps miles from the nearest service station, the noise of a sudden gasket problem can fool drivers into thinking they have a serious engine problem. The panic, although understandable, is largely unwarranted. The engine is not tearing itself apart, although it might sound that way. Most engine gasket problems have little or nothing to do with the immediate mechanical operation of a car. Certainly, the problem must be corrected at the first opportunity, but even with a blown engine gasket you can drive to a garage or filling station for a gasket replacement without damaging the engine.

Gaskets don't "blow," despite their reputation for doing so. Gaskets simply wear out. Gaskets are probably the most unmechanical things in your car. A gasket is simply a material— from cork to today's more exotic materials—used wherever two metal parts are joined and bolted together. If you try to pass oil, water, exhaust gases, or anything else through metal parts, they will leak because few (if any) parts can be mated perfectly. A gasket seals two imperfect surfaces. In filling the tiny void between joined parts, gaskets also act as sound suppressors.

Eventually, heat, pressure, age, and the action of whatever is flowing through the joined parts destroys a gasket's resiliency. The gasket develops cracks and breaks down. It no longer efficiently seals the space between the two parts. Replacement is the only cure.

Numerous types of gaskets seal and insulate car components. Exhaust manifold gaskets seal and deaden the sound of exhaust gases expelled from the engine. Oil pan gaskets prevent the leakage of engine oil from the reservoir under the chassis. Engine head gaskets pressure-seal and deaden sound at the joining of the engine's valve cover (where the valves are) and the lower part of the engine (where the cylinders are). They are often called cylinder head gaskets. Because of intense pressure and heat, these gaskets are the ones that most often fail.

➤ WHAT TO DO

1. Pull to the shoulder and stop. Switch off the engine.
2. Raise the hood and examine the area around the top of the engine. You'll probably see oil (evidence of a gasket leak).

3. To confirm your suspicion, start the engine and examine the top of the engine again. Small oil leaks may be more obvious. So may be wisps of smoke, as hot oil (which bathes the valves) leaks from the valve cover gasket and hits the hot engine.
4. The considerable noise alone should tell you it's the engine gasket. It's as though you can hear the combustion process going on inside the engine. And, in fact, if the gasket break is large enough, you can.
5. Despite the noise and minor leakage, the engine itself is largely unaffected by the gasket problem. The problem needs to be attended to, but the car is driveable. Drive (at reduced speed to hold down internal engine pressure) to the nearest garage or service station.

THE HOOD FLIES OPEN

You're driving in the highway's left lane when the hood flies open. Where, an instant before, you had clear and unobstructed vision of the way ahead, suddenly a metal barrier—the raised hood—totally obscures road vision. For all you can see, you might as well be blindfolded. But how did it happen?

Perhaps the hood latch hadn't been working right, but you neglected to have it fixed. Or maybe it hadn't been working at all, so you tied the hood shut with twine and it broke. Or perhaps, when you had the oil checked a few miles back, you or the attendant didn't close the hood forcefully enough.

➤ WHAT TO DO

1. Don't panic. Panic will rob you of the ability to think clearly and to do what you must do to avoid an accident.
2. Don't slam on the brakes. Other drivers may not be able to stop in time to avoid rear-ending you. Instead, lightly apply the brakes to alert cars behind that you are slowing down.
3. Quickly determine if you can peer under or around the upraised hood while you are driving. Often you can. By scrunching low in the seat you may be able to see the road through the gap between the raised hood and the cowling, just ahead of the windshield. If not, press your head against the driver-side window. Often this affords a view of the road if you remain in normal seating position.
4. If you still can't see under or around the hood, lower the driver-side window to gain a few inches of vision. Lean out a little, if you must. That should be enough to let you see around the edge of the hood.
5. With regained vision, signal a lane change, slow down, and make for the shoulder.
6. Get out of the car and close the hood. That may resolve the situation.
7. If the hood won't close or keeps opening (the latch may be broken or distorted), you've got to tie down the hood securely enough to drive to a garage or service station.

   If you don't have material to tie down the hood, you can "borrow" a piece of wire from somewhere in the car. For example, you can use a wire from one of the

If the hood flies open, you can usually still see the road ahead through the space beneath the upraised hood.

taillights (located in the trunk). True, you'll be driving with only one tail and brake light, but in your emergency that should be enough. What you cannot drive with is a hood that threatens to fly open at any moment.

8. Tying down the hood either with wire or stout cord isn't difficult if you keep one thing in mind: the material must be strong enough to firmly hold the hood in place. This will almost certainly mean several loops of wire or cord, not just one.

9. Tie one end of wire or cord to the hood latch or to one of the hood's metal supports and the other end through any convenient opening in the car's front end. Two or three loops with wire or cord, properly knotted, should keep the hood in place long enough to drive slowly to the nearest service shop for a permanent latch repair. Replace any car wiring you might have borrowed.

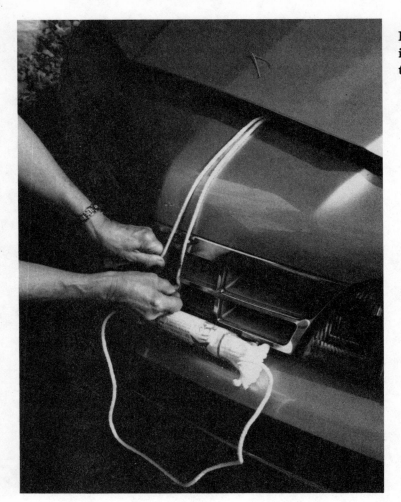

If the hood flies open, tie it shut until you can drive to a service station.

QUIET A STUCK HORN

While you're driving, without warning or apparent reason, your horn starts blaring. It's embarrassing, nerve-jangling, and even dangerous.

Is the horn button or steering wheel push pad or ring merely stuck, or is there a short circuit in the steering column, where the horn mechanism is? Perhaps the short circuit is in the horn's wiring under the hood (due to aged wires). Then again, the problem may be with the horn itself.

As the horn's cacophony drowns out the car radio, you really don't care what's wrong or where the trouble lies. You simply want to hush the horn.

➤ WHAT TO DO

1. Try the horn button or push pad. Push it, then release it. If the button or pad is merely stuck, as can happen, this may stop the blaring. If a couple of pushes doesn't work, you've got to try something else.
2. Slow down and, ever mindful of traffic around you, turn the steering wheel a little to the left and right. Depending on the make and model of your car, the horn's ON-OFF switch may be contained in the steering column, where some horn problems develop. Sometimes merely turning the wheel will temporarily cure the problem. If it doesn't, you have no choice but to pull to the shoulder or to the curb for a look under the hood.
3. Once you've stopped the car, shut off the engine and look under the hood.
4. Locate the horn. It is usually in the front, attached to one of the engine compartment's walls or frame members. Blaring as it is, it shouldn't be hard to locate. In cars with a pair of horns, the problem may be to locate which one is blaring.

   Most horns are energized by two wires connected to the battery. These wires usually carry only 12 volts of electricity (the same voltage it takes to power other car accessories) and present little danger of electrical shock. Even so, to quiet a horn you only handle one of the wires.
5. Now that you've located the horn and the two wires that make it sound, stick a rag in the horn to mute it while you work. Depending on how your horn is connected, cut one of the wires or simply unplug it where it connects with the horn. Doing

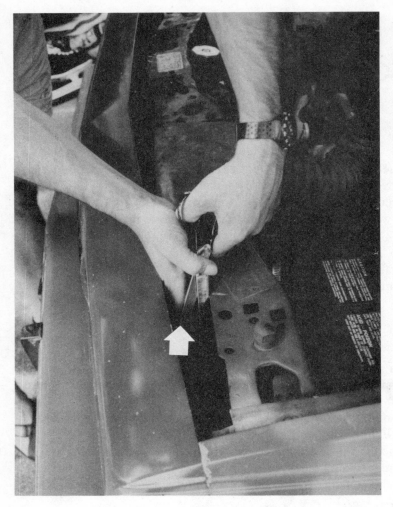

You can quiet some horns by pulling their electrical connection, by removing the fuse or switching off the breaker that energizes them, or by cutting one of their two electrical wires.

either cuts electrical energy to the horn and stills it. If you have two blaring horns, you'll have to unplug or cut a wire to each. Or you can remove the fuse to the circuit that powers the horns.

If you have the choice, pull the plug. Pulling it does no damage to a horn or its electrical wiring. When a mechanic repairs or installs a new horn, the wire will be replugged.

If you cut the wire, you do minor damage. A mechanic will have to replace the wire before repairing the horn. If the horn wires are old, a mechanic might replace them anyway. The replacement cost should be modest.

6. If you elect to cut a wire, use a knife, the wire-cutting jaws of a pair of pliers, a

scissors, or anything else with a cutting edge. Horn wires are usually small in diameter, not particularly strong, and easy to cut. Deprived of battery power, the horn will stop its blaring.

7. Whether you pull a wire or cut it, drive to an auto shop or, better, to a shop that specializes in automotive electrical problems, and have the horn fixed as soon as you can.

A TIRE GOES FLAT

Far more common than a steering tire blowout, which at high speeds may call for special maneuvering (see How to Survive a Front-Tire Blowout on page 199), is when a tire, usually punctured, simply loses its air and goes flat.

If it's a rear tire that goes flat, it may not affect steering, but the thumping sound of a flat tire is unmistakable. When a front steering tire goes flat, steering is harder and the car may veer in the direction of the flat. The reason for the veering is that the flat tire drags, pulling the steered wheels in its direction.

With a flat tire, either you've got to change to your spare, summon help to do it (perhaps your auto club, or the increasingly common road service offered by car manufacturers, or an independent tire changer), or elect to drive to the nearest service shop.

If you carry a flat-fix solution in the car (an aerosol sealer/inflator that can temporarily fix some flats), you may be able to seal a small hole (not a large puncture, sidewall damage, or valve or rim leaks) and inflate the tire sufficiently to drive to a service station. One warning: the propellant used in some sealer/inflators is highly flammable propane or butane. (Do not smoke while using these products.) When you reach a service shop, be sure to tell the tire repairer you used a tire sealer/inflator. The most effective aerosol sealer/inflators (get a 15-ounce or larger size, with a threaded hose that screws onto the tire's valve stem) work by propelling a water-soluble latex into the tire. Once the can's contents have been emptied into the tire (a process that usually takes several minutes), you're supposed to drive immediately to distribute the latex within the tire. This will temporarily repair the puncture. However, tire makers generally warn against these quick-fix remedies, contending that users may neglect to have the tire repaired.

Yet these aerosols can get your car to a repair shop when your own spare is underinflated (many often are), a tire tool or jack is missing or too hard to dig out of the trunk, or you simply don't want to hassle with a tire change.

➤ WHAT TO DO

For a flat at night on a highway:

1. Get off the road and onto the shoulder.
2. Changing the tire yourself, with traffic whizzing within a few feet, is dangerous. At

A tire with a small puncture can be temporarily inflated with an aerosol sealer/inflator.

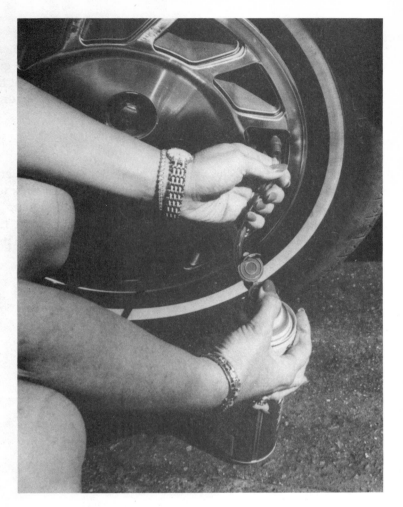

night, unless you have a flashlight and you're an experienced tire changer, or can summon one, you may decide to drive on the flat to a service station (assuming one is reasonably close).

3. Driving on a flat tire, if for only a few blocks, will almost certainly ruin the tire. If you must drive a considerable distance, the tire may actually come off and leave the metal rim. Still, the car is drivable if you proceed slowly, probably no faster than 10 to 15 mph, and if you keep firm steering control (a flat front tire affects steering).

4. If the distance to a service shop is too far to drive on a flat, you may have little choice but to change the tire yourself.

For a flat tire with no spare:

With no spare, a relatively routine flat can become an emergency. You can drive to the nearest service shop or get a tow truck to bring your car to a garage. You might even make arrangements with the tow-truck driver to return with a tire that fits your car, even a used tire. But this option is apt to be expensive. You are, after all, asking for services beyond the ordinary.

For a flat tire in town:

1. If you're an auto club member, phone for emergency service. A car manufacturer's road service may also be available. Or you might walk to a service station or garage and summon a repairman to install the spare. If you are close to a repair shop, you may choose to drive on the flat, regardless of probable tire damage.
2. Or you can change it yourself (see How to Change a Tire on page 185).

CHANGE A TIRE

Something goes bump, bump, bump. You stop, climb out, and see the expected. You've got a flat tire.

If you're near a phone, you can call your auto club. If not, you may have no choice but to change the tire yourself.

➤ WHAT TO DO

1. If you aren't out of traffic and on the shoulder, drive there—yes, even on the flat tire. Pick a level place for stability when jacking up the car.
2. Shut off the engine. Set the parking brake. Put the transmission in Park (for an automatic) or in gear (for a manual). Use flares or other warning devices (like reflective triangles). Turn on your four-way hazard flashers.
3. Get out the tire changing tools: a jack, a jack handle (to lower or raise the jack), and a lug wrench (the kind that resembles a cross is best) to remove the wheel's lug nuts (wheel nuts).
4. Remove the spare tire. In almost all cars you'll find it in the trunk, hidden under the trunk's floor mat.

   If you're driving a rental car, you may be in for a surprise. Some rental companies don't equip their cars with either spare tires or tire tools. Their reasoning: rental cars are all new. If a renter should have a flat, he or she can phone the rental office for help. With a fleet of thousands of cars, eliminating spare tires and tools saves big bucks. But it also puts rental clients at possible risk.

   Assuming you have a spare, you may still be in for a surprise. It may be a "compact tire"—a mere shadow of a normal-sized tire. A compact is designed for emergency use only. It restricts your road speed to 50 mph. If you're in snow country and you replace a drive tire with a compact, remember that you cannot put chains on a compact. Neither can you put your regular tire's wheel cover on a compact.

   If you don't have a spare, or if the compact is not inflated enough for safe highway-speed driving, you may have no choice but to drive slowly—no more than

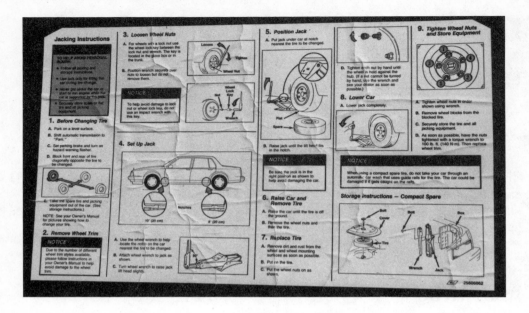

Complete jacking instructions, like this, are probably posted in the trunk. Instructions show jacking points and how to remove and replace a wheel and its wheel nuts.

10 to 15 mph—on the flat tire or underinflated compact to the nearest service station.

5. Minus any of these surprises, prepare to jack up the car. "Chock" (block) the wheel diagonally opposite from the wheel you intend to jack up. By chocking the wheel with a large rock, a log, or any other sturdy object, you prevent the car wheels from rolling while on the jack. (If the flat is in the rear, it's particularly important to chock both front tires, not just the one diagonally opposite the flat.)

6. If you don't know where the car's "jacking points" are, consult your owner's manual. Most jacking points are in the reinforced frame of the car, not the bumpers. Almost none of today's bumpers are strong enough for jacking.

Also, if your car has air suspension, before attempting to jack up a wheel you'll have to deactivate the suspension. Otherwise, it's often impossible to jack a car high enough off the ground to remove the wheel. For other types of suspensions, check your owner's manual to find the suspension deactivating switch. On some cars the switch is in the trunk.

7. Don't jack up the car until you remove the lug nuts. To do this, use the end of the jack handle or lug wrench to pry off the wheel cover (if the wheel cover is fastened by nuts, remove them first).

8. Using the lug wrench, loosen all the wheel nuts that hold the wheel in place. If a

wheel nut won't come loose, position the lug wrench firmly over the nut and step on the wrench's cross member. You may have to jump on the wrench to loosen very tight or rusted wheel nuts.

9. Wheel nuts loosened, jack up the car until the bottom of the flat tire is a few inches off the ground or pavement.
10. Remove the wheel nuts from their studs, removing the top one last. Keep the nuts together in the wheel cover so you won't lose them.
11. Lift off the flat tire, move it aside, and put the spare in its place. Engage the wheel on the top stud first, then on the other studs. Be sure the wheel is firmly in place. Replace and hand-tighten all of the wheel nuts, the top one last. When they are as tight as you can make them by hand, lower the jack until the wheel just touches the ground or pavement.
12. Using the lug wrench, begin tightening all of the wheel nuts. Tighten them in a criss-cross pattern—the top nut, then the bottom one, the left hand nut, then the right nut. Tighten them as firmly as you can, using both hands on the cross wrench. Then tighten them again.
13. Remove the jack, remove the wheel chocks, replace the wheel covers, put the flat tire, jack, and lug wrench in the trunk, and you're on your way.

With the wheel still on the ground, begin loosening the wheel cover's nuts.

Place the jack below the wheel's jacking point.

Remove all wheel nuts.

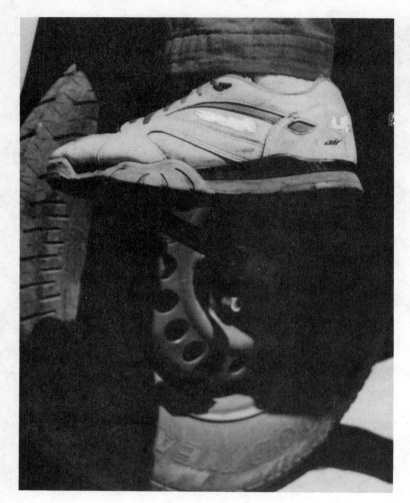

If the nuts are tight or rusted, you may have to step on the wrench handle to budge them.

Hang the spare from the top wheel lugs.

THE FRONT WHEELS
LOSE ALIGNMENT

You hit a curb too hard or are momentarily forced off the road and into the lane divider. As you steer back into traffic, there doesn't appear to be any real damage to your car.

But something has changed. The steering wheel wobbles in your grip and the car shimmies, worsening as you increase speed. Something is wrong with the front wheels, so you slow down (which decreases the wobbling), pull to the shoulder, and get out to have a look.

There is a slight dent and some scuff marks on the tires, but aside from this damage, you can see nothing seriously wrong. Yet something is wrong. The wheels are out of alignment.

Hitting a curb at even modest speed can throw the front wheels out of alignment.

This means that the front wheels are no longer able to track straight. Front-end accidents, even minor impacts, can cause misalignment. Front-end impacts can also bend wheels. These impacts can also damage the mechanism that controls the wheels and their steering—this damage may not be obvious upon casual front-wheel inspection.

➤ WHAT TO DO

1. Gauge the damage. It's likely the car is safe to drive, provided you don't drive very far. If you have a driving companion, have that person stand on the shoulder while you drive by slowly, to determine if the misalignment is modest or extreme.
2. Stay in the highway's right lane, or as close to the shoulder as feasible.
3. Drive at a modest speed to minimize vibration. This may mean driving 20 mph or slower. Be prepared to stop should things suddenly worsen.

A WHEEL BEARING FAILS

It begins with an obnoxious whine. The whine only worsens the farther you drive. The whining sound is coming from somewhere in front or behind, from a car extremity. And while the whining may grow more persistent and louder at higher speeds, it may not grow—at first—that much worse. Whatever the sound, a wheel bearing is grinding toward failure.

All four wheels have bearings. Your car's wheels rotate on them. Almost always they are roller bearings, and they need periodic inspection and greasing. When a mechanic greases or "packs" the bearings, he or she dips a finger into a can of grease and smears it liberally over the wheel bearings. Wheel bearings for most cars should be inspected, if not repacked, twice a year. To inspect them, the car is hoisted or the wheels jacked off the ground. The mechanic spins each wheel to see if it turns freely and listens for the sounds—grating or rubbing—of a wheel bearing that is installed too tightly or too loosely, or needs replacement.

A failing bearing is not a signal that a wheel is going to fall off. It does mean, however, that the bearing has to be repacked or, more likely, replaced. If the rollers of a wheel bearing are chipped, cracked, scored, or broken, the bearing needs replacement.

When a wheel bearing fails, it can affect how the car handles and drives. A defective, overheated bearing can slow a wheel and bind it so that the car tends to steer hard or fight the direction you're steering.

➤ WHAT TO DO

1. Pinpoint where the trouble is. Since a bearing whines only when the wheel is turning, you'll have to drive the car to tell which wheel is affected. Have a companion listen for the noise as you slowly drive by (then drive in the other direction to check the other side of the car).
2. When you have identified which wheel bearing needs attention, plot a route to the nearest repair shop or service station.
3. Driving slowly reduces friction on the bearing and makes it easier to steer if the bearing is causing the wheel to drag or fight your steering.

A "listener" pinpoints the
wheel with the failing
bearing.

A wheel bearing.

YOU LOSE A WHEEL WHILE DRIVING

If you lose a wheel while driving, it's apt to be because its lug nuts (which hold the wheel to the axle by way of the brake housing) were not securely tightened. That's why you should inspect your car when you have new tires installed or a flat fixed, before you drive out of the shop.

If something is wrong, you may be able to spot it. For example, if the wheel is supposed to be secured with six lug nuts and you count only three or four, something is definitely wrong. The boltlike threaded studs that stick out from the wheel mount should have a lug nut screwed onto each of them.

Mechanic neglect is not the only reason you may lose a wheel. Metal fatigue is another. Bolts can weaken with age and break. Hitting a highway divider or a road obstacle at high speed may also cause a car to lose a wheel.

If your car loses a wheel, you're in for a fight to keep the car on the road, let alone in its driving lane. Sometimes the car loses all or some of its braking power (depending on the car's make and model) because a hydraulic brake line is severed. Lose a rear wheel, and you may still have steering. Lose a front wheel and you may not.

➤ WHAT TO DO

If you lose a rear wheel:

1. Take your foot off the gas pedal, braking hard to slow yourself, if you can.
2. Don't head for the shoulder. Whether you lose a front or rear wheel, you may not have enough steering control to get there safely.
3. Steer in whatever direction you must to keep the car going straight. This may mean momentarily steering in the opposite direction of the skid, rather than in its direction, as you would for virtually every other type of skid.
4. If it's a right rear wheel you've lost, the car will tend to swerve to the right; if a left rear wheel, to the left. Assuming the pavement is dry, steer in the opposite direction to correct the swerve and to prevent the car from changing lanes.

5. Even if you've lost some or all braking power, the dragging rear axle will brake the car, although slowly. Aid braking by downshifting into a lower gear.
6. Get the car stopped as soon as you can to prevent additional damage. Much of the rear body, especially on the side of the lost wheel, may be dragging on the pavement, damaging and crumpling body metal. There's even a possibility of gas tank damage or rupture.

If you lose a front wheel:

1. As the car nosedives and tilts, either left or right, steer to keep it tracking straight. Lose a front wheel at high speed and a car may pivot around the axle that's on the pavement. Only hard opposite direction steering can avoid a potential spin.
2. As you fight for control, brake hard. You've got to stop before you lose total control.
3. Lose a front wheel, and you could lose power steering, making it all but impossible to steer. (Steering is hard enough if you lose power steering with front wheels intact.) In transaxle, front-wheel drive cars that have added weight upfront, loss of power steering further increases steering difficulty.
4. If you lose a front wheel, it is possible to also lose your brakes. Downshift to a lower gear; use the engine as a brake.
5. Get the car stopped as soon as possible to prevent further damage, especially to fenders, the bumper, and body metal in the front of the car.

HOW TO

SURVIVE A FRONT-TIRE BLOWOUT

There's a bang from the front of your car—maybe louder than any sound you've ever heard—and the steering wheel threatens to wrestle itself from your grip. You've had a front-tire blowout.

➤ WHAT TO DO

1. Steer straight. Maintain your lane position.
2. Take your foot off the gas pedal.
3. If the steering wheel vibrates violently in your hands, grip it tighter and force the car to drive straight.
4. Don't let the noise panic you (the flat tire may flap and/or the metal rim may scrape on the pavement).
5. Brake slowly, enough to reduce speed but not so much as to cause the car to veer. When a front steering tire goes flat, a car tends to pull in the direction of the blow-out. Hard braking may make the veering more pronounced. Continue to brake gently.
6. Hold the wheel straight as you slow down. Don't prematurely head for the shoulder for fear of ruining your tire. If it blew, the tire is already beyond repair.
7. When you've slowed sufficiently, signal traffic of your intention to head for the shoulder.
8. Once you've stopped on the shoulder, put the transmission in Park or the shift in gear, set the parking brake, and shut off the engine. Don't touch the blown tire until it has cooled. The rubber, even the rim, may be too hot to touch.
9. Put on the spare tire. Since there's no predicting when a tire will go flat or blow out, at the first opportunity you'll have to buy another new or used tire.

A front-tire blowout.

THE ASHTRAY CATCHES ON FIRE

Your car's ashtray isn't a wastebasket, but some people use it as one. A match or a stubbed-out cigarette can ignite its trash. The smoldering ashtray can suddenly burst into flame.

Even though the blazing ashtray may not set the car on fire, its flames and heat can singe, even burn, the vinyl, plastic, or leather instrument panel or armrest trim surrounding it. You've got to put out the fire before it does damage.

➤ WHAT TO DO

1. Don't panic. But do act fast.
2. Smother the flames by using the ashtray's own cover, lid, or fireproof recess.
3. If it's the type of ashtray that slides into a fireproof recess, shove it in all the way. That alone should deprive the flames of oxygen and snuff the fire out. If the ashtray has a hinged top or lid, shut the top tight. That, too, should smother the flames. Again, no oxygen, no fire.
4. Smothering an ashtray fire isn't always achieved quickly. Several minutes may pass before the oxygen-starved flames wither and finally go out.

   You can speed up the process if you "blanket" the closed or recessed ashtray. For example, you can hold an old denim jacket or trousers tightly over the ashtray lid or recess opening to shut out air.
5. There are other ways to put out an ashtray fire, but they tend to be messy and less efficient than smothering. Almost any liquid—soda, water, even beer—can be used to put the fire out. But resort to dousing only if smothering doesn't get quick results.

   Avoid the temptation to remove a burning ashtray. Aflame, they are often too hot to handle. You might spill the tray's flaming contents in the car.

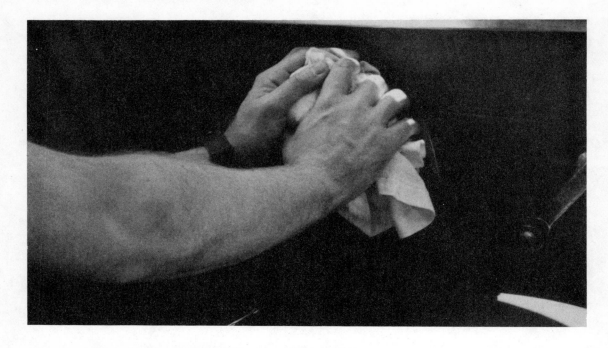

To starve a fire, hold a folded rag over the shut ashtray.

THE CONVERTIBLE TOP SUDDENLY RAISES

Perhaps you were in a hurry to lower your car's convertible top and didn't latch it securely. Or, maybe you simply neglected to have a defective latch repaired.

Then it happens when you least expect it. While speeding on a freeway, the top suddenly raises.

➤ WHAT TO DO

1. Don't brake in panic. Concentrate on steering. The car may veer suddenly, left or right, as wind catches and buffets the raised, nearly vertical top, as if it were a sail.
2. Slow cautiously. For the moment, ignore the top.
3. Make no attempt, at any speed, to reach up or out to lower it. You won't succeed. Try, and the wind could drag you right out of the driver's seat.
4. As you slow down, switch on your four-way hazard flashers and check traffic behind, if you can. You probably can't if your top is like most when raised; vision through the rearview mirror will be totally blocked. Vision through the side mirrors may be partially or completely blocked, too. You may have to adjust the driver-side mirror for a broader view of the road behind.
5. Get onto the shoulder.
6. Once stopped, climb out to check for any damage. The wind may have bent or distorted the top's frame or the mechanism that raises and lowers it. The top's fabric may also be torn.
7. See if you can lower the top. If it resists, you'll have to force it down. Some tops can be dismantled for temporary storage, in the backseat, for example.
8. Once the top is lowered, see if it will lock.
9. If it won't lock, and even if it will (don't trust its locking mechanism until you can have it checked), tie it down until you can have it fixed. If you don't have rope or wire to tie it with, use your belt or shoelaces, or a nonessential wire from the car (a taillight wire, for example).
10. If you can't tie the top down, you'll have to hold it down with your left hand (while you steer with the right) until you can get to a repair shop.

Never attempt to hold down the top once it has begun to raise.

**Stop and examine the
latch on your convertible.**

AN ENGINE MOUNT BREAKS

As you come to a screeching, tire-smoking stop on the highway (for example, in an effort to avoid rear-ending a car stopped dead in your lane), you hear a clunking noise. Or maybe you hear it when trying to extricate the wheels from a soft-shoulder sand trap, you gun the engine hard—maybe too hard—in reverse.

You may not even hear the clunk above the sound of your fast-revving engine or the screech of your tires, but you feel the results. Your car shakes violently and keeps shaking as you drive on. You may conclude that the car has a damaged automatic transmission because the shaking increases as you drive at higher speeds. But as you shift through the transmission's gears, you may find they function properly, although the noise and shaking continue. It's not the transmission. There's a problem with the engine mounts.

One or more (likely several) mounts have been broken or loosened by hard braking or reversing too fast. The engine mounts (often called "motor mounts") are no longer doing what they are supposed to do: holding the engine fixed to the car's frame.

An engine may be held to the car's frame by a few engine mounts (never less than two) or by a number of them. They are inexpensive engine position-holders, but absolutely essential. If they break, which is not unusual, the engine is free to move. If you stop suddenly when an engine is no longer tethered by its motor mounts, the engine can slide forward (in a rear-drive car) and shove its fast-spinning fan through the radiator. Wobbling and untethered, it can do other major damage under the hood—for example, major damage to the transmission.

A car may not even shake or make noise when a motor mount loosens or breaks. That's what's so insidious about motor-mount breakage. You can break all of the mounts except one and hardly notice the difference. But break the remaining mount and the engine, no longer held in its proper place, becomes a loose cannon under the hood.

➤ WHAT TO DO

1. Pull to the shoulder and stop.
2. Go through the gears again, if only to prove to yourself that the transmission is all right.
3. Then, with the hand brake set (and the transmission in Park for automatics), keep the engine idling and lift the hood.

4. Carefully observe the engine in operation. You may be able to detect some engine movement, as though it were no longer anchored to the engine compartment. However, more than likely, you will not be able to see the motor mounts because they are usually beneath the engine.

5. If you want to confirm the problem, shut off the engine and use a stout stick, a board, or the jack's handle as a prying tool. Wedge it under the engine and push upwards. If the engine wobbles, it is no longer held firmly to the car's frame.

6. Whether on the highway or street, you can drive to the nearest repair shop—provided you drive slowly and drive defensively. Avoid sudden braking or acceleration. Doing either may cause the engine to move, either forward or backward and possibly to one side or the other. An engine loose under the hood is something you definitely don't want.

7. Have a mechanic replace or repair the engine mount(s). It is a relatively quick and inexpensive job.

THE TRANSMISSION BEGINS TO FAIL

When transmissions (both manual and automatic) fail, they can go fast, with a "pffft" and a cloud of smoke. Or, they can falter: you put the shift in Park and it slips into Reverse, or the transmission works fine in Drive but not in a lower gear. Often transmission trouble is signaled by a pause (most obvious when you start the car on a cold morning). For example, when you shift into Drive, there may be a pause. Slippage is another sign. When you shift between First and Second, or the transmission self-shifts on a hill, it slips, as if suddenly disconnected from the wheels, and the engine races.

When a transmission fails, it is not necessarily due to old age. By design, a transmission should last the life of your car's engine. More often, transmission failure is the car owner's fault. Either an owner fails to maintain the transmission fluid at its proper level or overfills that level. Transmissions are particularly sensitive to overfilling. Neglected routine maintenance is certainly the largest cause of premature transmission failure. To find out how often your car's transmission should be serviced and its transmission fluid changed, see your owner's manual.

But can you drive to a garage if the transmission fails or begins to fail on a highway? If it suddenly and totally fails without warning, and the car will not move or the transmission will not respond or shift in any gear, you will have to be towed. Total transmission failure is one of the few car and driving emergencies for which there is no quick fix.

But if the transmission slips or just won't operate in drive, you may still be able to drive to a repair shop.

➤ WHAT TO DO

1. Put the transmission in Park, leave the engine running, lift the hood, and check the transmission fluid level. Transmission fluid is checked with the engine operating.

   For an accurate reading, most carmakers recommend that transmission fluid be checked at normal operating temperature (if you've been driving fast, in hot weather, or in heavy traffic, wait 15 to 30 minutes before checking the fluid level) and that the car be parked on a level place.

2. Withdraw the dipstick from the transmission fill pipe, wipe the stick with a rag or tissue, then reinsert it as deep as it will go in the fill pipe. Wait a few seconds, then carefully withdraw the dipstick and examine where the fluid level is on *both* sides of

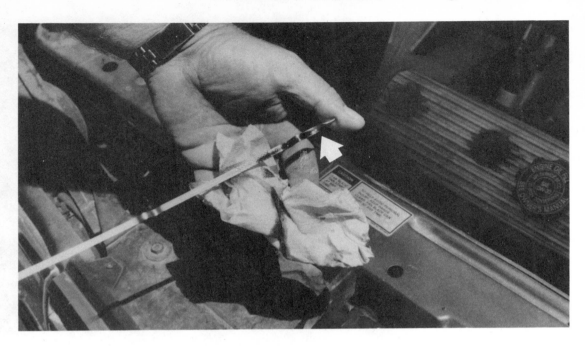

If the transmission fluid level is not dangerously low, you can drive slowly to the nearest service station.

the dipstick. Usually, a crosshatched area will indicate the correct level. If the fluid level is below this area, there's not enough fluid; if above it, the transmission is overfilled.

3. If the fluid level is low, that may be the cause of the transmission's slippage or failure to shift. There is an area on most dipsticks that indicates when a fluid level is so low that driving almost any distance at almost any speed risks transmission damage. Unless the transmission has a major leak or you've neglected checking the fluid level for too long, a fluid level that low is rare.

In checking the fluid level, you may notice that the transmission fluid is brownish and smells burned or that it is a milky pinkish color and seems to contain air bubbles. All of these are symptoms of possible transmission trouble (the milky color usually indicates water has gotten into the transmission; the bubbles, that there's an air leak in a transmission hose).

4. If the fluid level is all right, test the transmission to see if it will shift and operate; try Drive or any lower gear. It may, for example, get the car moving in Second gear but not in Drive. Unless the fluid level is dangerously low, the car can be driven slowly in Second gear—or even in a lower gear if the transmission will shift into it.

(Many automatic transmissions default to Second gear when they fail, enabling you to continue to drive, albeit slowly.)

5. Even if the fluid level is low, but not dangerously so, you can drive slowly to the nearest service station (the transmission may continue to behave erratically). Adding the transmission fluid recommended for your car may cure your transmission problem.

THE DRIVE SHAFT BREAKS

You're driving in town when the car suddenly loses all speed and power and, as if engineless, comes to a stop. If there is a warning, it comes simultaneously—perhaps a clattering under the chassis (for a rear-wheel-drive car) or the sound of mangling metal (for a front-wheel drive).

Oddly, there seems to be nothing wrong with the engine or with the transmission or gears. When you press the gas pedal, the engine revs, as if raring to go. But when you attempt to shift the transmission, the car won't respond.

The drive shaft, which delivers the engine's power through the gears or transmission to the wheels, has broken. Since no power is being delivered to the wheels, the car stops.

On rear-wheel-drive cars with long drive shafts, the shaft may actually wrestle loose and drag on the pavement. Front-wheel-drive cars have only a short drive shaft between transmission and front drive wheels. But if the drive shaft is broken, the result is the same: no power to the wheels.

A broken drive shaft is one of the few driving emergencies that a driver cannot, by will or wile, extricate himself or herself from.

➤ WHAT TO DO

Call a tow truck. There is little else you can do.

THE LOW-OIL LIGHT FLASHES ON

A car's instrument panel, whether classic gauges and dials or "idiot lights" (warning lights that come on when trouble is indicated), can signal an imminent emergency—or far less. A "low oil" warning, however it's displayed on the instrument panel, *is* an emergency.

It may indicate you've gone several months without checking the oil level. Normal car usage and small leaks, not unusual in older engines, can deplete the engine's reservoir of oil to the danger point.

It may indicate an instrument problem. The oil gauge or trouble indicator can give a false reading if there's an electrical short or some other instrument or electrical malfunction.

It may indicate an internal engine problem. The engine, whose very life depends on constant lubrication, may be suffering from lack of lubrication. Starved for oil, the engine may "seize"—its hot, fast-moving parts may become welded together. When an oil-starved engine seizes, it self-destructs.

Even if it does not seize and stop, an oil-deprived engine's microfine moving surfaces may begin to chafe and erode. Driving on critically low oil for five minutes can shear years from an engine's useful life.

➤ WHAT TO DO

1. Stop immediately. If traffic permits, put the transmission or gear in Neutral to reduce engine speed to idle (its functional minimum operating speed) and coast to a stop on the shoulder. If possible, try to pick a level place on the shoulder when you stop. This will give a more accurate reading of the engine's oil level when you test it.
2. Turn off the engine.
3. Lift the hood and locate the engine's oil-measuring dipstick. Withdraw the dipstick, wipe it clean, and reinsert it in the dipstick tube. Push the dipstick down as far as it will go in the tube. Then carefully withdraw it again so as not to smear the dipstick with oil from the sides of the tube, which can result in a false reading.
4. Retest 15 to 20 minutes later, allowing time for oil to drain into the crank case. If both readings are identical—just the tip of the stick is wet—your engine has very little oil but probably enough to drive a very short distance (very slowly) to a service station.

Easy-to-read oil fill and dipstick location labels.

If the dipstick shows no indication of oil at all, the oil is too low to risk even starting the engine.

5. Whether or not to risk a slow drive to the nearest service station—assuming *some* oil shows on the dipstick—rests largely on whether the low oil level is the result of your oversight or a fault in the engine and its components. Try to recall when you last checked or had the oil level checked.

6. If you carry a spare quart or two of engine oil, add a quart after removing the engine oil filler cap. Dipstick-test the oil level again. If it indicates a normal level, or at least a far higher level than before you added the quart, you can breathe easier: the low-oil level was probably not due to an engine problem.

   With the oil level restored to normal, you can drive the car. But stop every 50 miles (if on the highway) to recheck the oil level, and check it for a few days.

7. If you don't carry spare oil, or if you recently filled the oil but the dipstick shows a shortage of oil, your decision whether or not to drive to a nearby service station becomes more critical. There is obviously an engine or component problem.

   Can you risk even a short drive? Most experts say yes—provided you stop every mile to recheck the oil level. If the dipstick reading remains constant, continue . . . slowly.

   If, when rechecking, the dipstick comes up dry, stop and turn off the engine. Drive even a minute longer and you will almost certainly destroy the engine.

THE AIR-BAG LIGHT
OR BEEPER STAYS ON

The instrument panel's air-bag alert flashes on and stays on. If your car's "trouble-circuit" is also programmed to sound an alert, the beeper joins the light in pinpointing an apparent emergency.

But there is no real emergency, certainly not what a car owner would view as a driving emergency. Nor does this alert demand the kind of decisive action necessary to extricate yourself from a life-threatening road confrontation.

Yet many drivers, suddenly alerted to an air-bag problem, believe they are somehow in imminent danger and that at any moment the air bag will inflate in their faces. Some, startled by a bag alert, abandon their cars to a tow truck, certain that their cars are undriveable.

Studies of spontaneous, noncollision air bag inflations show that these incidents are exceedingly rare. In one insurance company study of some 75,000 air-bag inflations, fewer than half a dozen were blamed on inadvertent, noncollision inflation. All the rest inflated in response to collisions. Insurance companies make it their business to investigate the causes of air-bag inflations because they pay the considerable cost of replacing air bags inflated during collisions.

What emergency, then, does a driver face when the dashboard's visual or audible air-bag alert goes off? Actually, none. All the alert signals is that there is a fault in the air-bag deployment circuit, and that, for your own safety in case of some future accident, you should have the trouble checked and corrected at your earliest opportunity.

But some carmakers do nothing to allay people's fears. Quite the opposite. In some cars the beeper continues to beep periodically, convincing drivers not only that an emergency exists, but that whatever is wrong needs immediate correction.

➤ WHAT TO DO

1. Don't panic, as do many drivers. There is no emergency, nor much chance of premature air-bag inflation. The alert light signals only that the air-bag system needs professional checking. The beeper, additionally, may indicate that the alert light has malfunctioned or has simply burned out.
2. Continue driving. There is no need to stop, since there is nothing to examine and

nothing that can be done short of professional servicing. Remind yourself, however, to have the air-bag system checked.

3. If your bag system has a beeper or chime that sounds periodically and is annoying to listen to, you can silence it by removing the fuse that energizes the alert's circuit. Removing the fuse won't deactivate the air bag or impair its response in any way.

   To locate the correct fuse, and the location of your car's fuse box, consult your owner's manual. Typically, the air-bag alert circuit shares the same fuse with several other accessories. Removing the bag's fuse may, for example, also defuse the windshield heater, the car's level control, and perhaps one or two other usually minor accessories. If you feel you can drive comfortably and safely without them, remove the fuse until you can have the bag system repaired.

AN INSTRUMENT PANEL ALERT FLASHES

Does an instrument panel's alert—or a gauge pointer's sudden moving into a warning zone—signal a real and imminent emergency?

Some warning lights flash on briefly during routine start-up to indicate a car's operational status. For example, when you turn the key in the ignition but have not yet started the engine, the battery charging alert may go on. Since the engine is not yet running, the battery has not begun to charge. The moment the engine is started, which charges the battery, the alert should go off.

Other alerts flash briefly simply to show systems are working. On some cars, when you turn the ignition to the start position, the oil level alert briefly flashes, indicating that the alert system is working properly and that its bulb has not burned out. Some other alerts tell you when something needs routine attention—such as the dashboard's SERVICE ENGINE SOON warning.

Alerts by themselves do not necessarily signal an emergency situation. A driver must interpret the alert along with other visual or audible indications of trouble. An engine coolant alert may only indicate that coolant temperature is too hot. An emergency may not exist unless you hear steam hissing under the hood.

Here's a rundown of what instrument alerts usually mean, and how to deal with them. In all cases, however, check your owner's manual for special instrument-alert instructions.

Oil Warning Alert

What it means: a probable emergency situation. If it flashes and stays on, or if the gauge shows low pressure, there is too little oil, the oil pressure is too low, or oil flow is not cooling or properly lubricating the engine. Both alerts may also signal other oil-related problems.

➤ WHAT TO DO

1. Immediately check the oil level.
2. If the oil level is all right, there may be a serious oil or lubrication problem. See a mechanic immediately.

Check Oil Level Alert

What it means: not yet an emergency situation. But you're running low on oil. Indicates that the engine oil level is one to one and a half quarts low.

➤ **WHAT TO DO**

Check the oil level. Add oil until the dipstick shows the proper operational level.

Battery Alert or Gauge's Pointer Shows No Charging or Discharge

What it means: a pending emergency. Your battery isn't being charged. You won't be able to drive very long, especially at night when you use the headlights, if the battery isn't being charged or is being drained.

➤ **WHAT TO DO**

1. Have your battery and its system (alternator, drive belt, voltage regulator, cables, and connections) checked at the first opportunity. Meanwhile, turn off everything that uses battery power: the radio, the heater or air conditioner, anything not absolutely necessary. Refrain from turning off the engine and having to restart it. The starter motor is usually a car's single largest drainer of battery power.
2. If driving at night, stop at a service station while you still have enough power for the headlights.

Service Engine Soon Alert

What it means: usually not an emergency. You probably have an engine problem, but not necessarily a serious or costly one.

➤ **WHAT TO DO**

Take the car into a service shop for a checkup.

Low Coolant Warning

What it means: not an emergency. The coolant level in the radiator is low.

➤ **WHAT TO DO**

1. Check the radiator's coolant level.
2. Add the proper amount of water/antifreeze so the coolant level returns to normal. A service station attendant can determine if the water/antifreeze ratio is correct.

Brake System Alert

What it means: a possible emergency, but often not. Some cars have at least two braking systems. If one goes out, you can still brake, although usually not as well. Even if the brake pedal sinks to the floorboard, you can probably revive braking enough to get to a mechanic.

➤ **WHAT TO DO**

1. Have your brakes and the hydraulic fluid reservoirs checked at the very first opportunity.
2. For reviving failing or fading brakes see What to Do if the Brakes Suddenly Fail on page 139.

Low Washer Fluid Alert

What it means: no emergency. The fluid in the windshield washer reservoir is low.

➤ **WHAT TO DO**

The next time you pull into a service station, check the washer's fluid level and fill the reservoir with washer fluid to the proper level.

Antilock Brake Warning

What it means: generally, not an emergency. Either your car's antilock braking system is no longer working or has a problem. You can drive without antilock braking. But if both the antilock and regular brake alerts go on, the car's brakes may be failing.

➤ **WHAT TO DO**

1. If both systems are out, try to revive braking sufficiently to drive slowly to a garage, brake specialist, or to your car dealer.

2. For reviving fading or failed brakes see What to Do if the Brakes Become Wet and Fail on page 33.

Low-Fuel Alert or Gauge on Empty

What it means: only an emergency if you permit the car to run out of gas.

➤ WHAT TO DO

1. Stop at the next filling station for gas, even if it means leaving the highway.
2. If you run out of gas see How to Fill a Gas Tank from a Tote Can on page 73.

Traction Control System Warning

What it means: usually not an emergency situation by itself. The car's wheel-spin control system isn't working. You can usually do without traction control, which limits wheel spin on icy or wet roads, or when you're bogged down in sand, snow, or mud. But the traction control may also indicate an overheated transaxle (the axle/transmission in front-wheel-drive cars), overheated brakes, and other problems.

➤ WHAT TO DO

1. Have the traction control system checked and serviced at your earliest opportunity.
2. If the alert flashes and stays on, the problem may be more than the traction system. Take the car to your dealer as soon as you can.

THE CIGARETTE LIGHTER STICKS AND GROWS HOT

You push in the cigarette lighter. The ON indicator, if it has one, flicks red. You wait for the lighter to pop out. But it doesn't. It is stuck in its socket. Try as you will, you can't get the lighter out and you can't shut it off. It is too hot to handle bare-handed.

➤ WHAT TO DO

1. First, insulate your fingers with a rag or several layers of handkerchief. Give it another few tries—twisting and turning it as you pull.
2. If that fails, try to remove it with a pair of pliers. If you use vise-grip pliers, be careful not to apply too much force. The tool may distort the lighter, making removal even harder, if not impossible.
3. If you are still unable to remove it, you can simply wait for it to burn out. Most car lighters aren't designed for prolonged operation. In time, they overheat and burn out. There should be no danger of fire. (Most lighter sockets are well insulated from their automotive surroundings.)
4. There is, however, one simple way to shut the lighter off before it self-destructs: remove the fuse or deactivate the circuit breaker that energizes the lighter's electrical circuit. To find the fuse or breaker that controls electricity to the lighter, consult your car owner's manual. Removing the lighter's fuse or tripping its breaker shuts off the lighter. *But,* because your lighter may also share the same electrical circuit as your car's horn (in some cars), turning off the lighter may also turn off the horn. The horn won't work until you replace the fuse or close the breaker.

In time, overheated lighter coils will burn out.

THE POWER STEERING SUDDENLY FAILS

Something is wrong. You feel it in the steering wheel. One moment you have power steering and the next you don't, or power steering is fading away gradually: little by little it becomes harder to steer.

The car's loss of power steering may announce itself with a squeal and a tangle of noise, or with a dry sound, as if something needs lubrication. Then again, the trouble may begin with an acrid smell, even wisps of smoke curling up from the hood.

Those sounds and smells, along with the steering wheel's gradual or sudden stiffening, point to several mechanical problems that prelude loss of power steering. The squeal is likely the result of the power-steering pump drivebelt working loose from the engine-driven pulley that powers it, or from a broken drivebelt. The dry sound may be due to a leak in the power-steering unit or in the high-pressure hose that has all but emptied the power-steering pump sump of its vital lubricant—power-steering fluid. The pump's fast-turning rotor is spinning unlubricated. The acrid smell and wisps of smoke are far more worrisome: almost certainly the power-steering high-pressure hose has sprung a leak, spewing power-steering fluid on the hot engine.

➤ WHAT TO DO

1. Grip the steering wheel tightly with both hands, to maintain as much steering control as you can. To do so, you may have to exert more strength than you've ever needed for steering before.
2. Keep the car's wheels rolling, as you plan how to get off the highway or to the side of the street. Don't make the mistake—a natural reaction—of braking hard to slow down or stop. Slowing suddenly in traffic is not only dangerous, but makes steering even harder without power-steering power. Keep the wheels rolling as you gently brake, reducing your speed.
3. If you can momentarily spare a hand from the wheel, switch on your "flashers"— hazard lights—as a warning to drivers behind and ahead that you're in trouble. The trouble you're in, while vexing, isn't really all that serious. But it may test both your

strength and good humor before you find a garage or filling station where you can have the problem taken care of.

4. Once you pull to the shoulder or side of the street, stop and have a look under the hood before you decide your next move. In today's component-crowded engines, you may have trouble locating the broken power-steering belt or the leaky high-pressure power-steering hose and its leak.

    If it's a broken drivebelt, and you can reach it, untangle it from wherever it's tangled and remove it. The broken belt can't be repaired. When you get to a garage, you'll need a new belt.

    If it's a leak in the power-steering high-pressure fluid hose, and you have a roll of duct tape, a few windings of tape around the leak should permit you to drive to a service station (see How to Quick-Fix a Power-Steering Hose Leak on page 166) provided you have been successful in stopping the leak from the power-steering hose. If you can't fix it, you're stuck. You can't risk driving with power-steering fluid splattering the hot engine. That could start a fire under the hood.

    If it's not a hose leak, or if it is and you managed to stop it, none of the other power-steering problems will render the car undriveable.

5. Even without power steering, you can drive to the nearest repair shop, although your car will be harder to steer. Drive at slow to modest speeds, anticipating curves or other road variances that require excessive steering. If possible, take a less-trafficked route. As difficult as your car will be to steer, you don't need an added hazard—traffic.

WHAT TO DO IN

A TOTAL ELECTRICAL FAILURE

Without warning, your car suffers a total electrical failure. Everything energized by the battery, including onboard electronics, the engine (its spark plugs are electrically fired), and all the lights—including headlights—go out.

There's no right or sure way to extricate yourself and your car from so complete and catastrophic a failure. When a car's electrical system totally fails, which is rare, virtually everything quits. You should, however, still have operating brakes, but not powered ones. You'll also lose power steering.

➤ **WHAT TO DO**

If you have a total electrical failure on a highway:

1. Shift quickly into Neutral to maintain coasting speed.
2. Brake so that you slow from highway speed to between 35 to 40 mph. Without engine power, you need to coast to reach the shoulder.
3. Signal your intent to change lanes (if you're in a center or left lane), or to steer for the shoulder. Without turn indicators, you'll have to use hand signals. But if you have power windows and they're closed, you won't be able to put a hand out to signal. Hold up a hand and hope that the driver behind you recognizes your signal from inside the car.
4. On the shoulder, without any warning lights, you have little choice but to raise the hood, put out flares, reflective triangles, or signal your distress by flashlight, and wait for a highway patrol car or tow truck to stop. If you have a self-powered car phone or can safely reach a freeway call box, phone for help.
5. With the hood raised, look for the problem. Sometimes one of the battery's clamps and its electrical cable (usually the positive clamp and cable) become loose or dislodged from their battery post. If so, the problem can easily be fixed. With a wrench, replace or tighten the clamp on its battery post. This may restore the car's power and extricate you from the emergency.

At night on a highway or rural road:

1. Continue to steer straight, as you did before the blackout, assuming you're traveling on a straight road.
2. Brake to slow down, but not so much as to eliminate coasting, and shift into Neutral.
3. Envision what the road ahead looked like, the position of traffic, and any shoulder obstructions as they existed moments before the road blacked out.
4. Steer toward the shoulder (or where the shoulder should be). Prepare for a quick stop.
5. Brace yourself for a possible crash. Keep a firm grip on the wheel.
6. When you believe you have reached the shoulder—it's likely you won't be able to see it unless oncoming car lights illuminate the road—brake hard to stop quickly, mindful of following traffic (if any).

THE FAN BELT BREAKS OR LOOSENS

A coolant warning on the dashboard or the distinctive smell and sight of steam hissing from a hot radiator are indications of a broken fan belt. (Some of today's cars don't have any belts because the radiator's cooling fan is powered electrically.) If your car doesn't have a fan belt, you may have a multidrive "serpentine" belt. The single, long serpentine belt—so called because it snakes from one accessory drive pulley to another—may power almost every accessory under the hood once driven by a myriad of "dedicated" belts—belts designed to drive a single accessory. A single serpentine belt may drive the power-steering pump, the battery-charging alternator, the air conditioner's compressor, the water pump, and even the radiator fan unless it is electrically powered.

A conventional fan belt might break without your knowledge until the engine overheats. Not so with a serpentine belt. When it breaks or slips off its pulleys, you know it instantly because you lose anywhere from several to half a dozen driving accessories—power steering being one of them. These failures, or even one of them, are often a tip-off that the radiator fan (probably driven by the serpentine belt) is no longer cooling the radiator. Before the radiator overheats, you have to take steps to avoid being stranded on the highway with a boiling radiator.

➤ **WHAT TO DO**

1. Pull to the shoulder and stop immediately.
2. Don't turn off the engine. Let the engine idle. If you turn the engine off, residual engine heat may unnecessarily overheat the radiator's coolant, something you don't want to let happen.
3. Raise the hood to see if the radiator fan is still turning. If the serpentine belt is broken, the fan won't be turning. *Caution:* Be absolutely certain how your car's radiator fan is driven before you stick your hand under the hood. If it is electrically powered, the fan can begin to turn without warning in response to a change in coolant temperature. If you have your hands anywhere near an electrically powered radiator fan, and it suddenly goes into operation, you can be seriously hurt.
4. Loosen or remove the radiator cap (or flip the pressure-release switch, if your car has one). Doing so depressurizes the radiator system, normally maintained at high pres-

Fan belts are all but obsolete. The radiator fan is electrically driven, or powered by a "serpentine" belt.

sure by the cap. With the pressure relieved, the radiator's coolant will heat much more slowly, giving you a few more minutes of emergency driving.

5. Close the hood, *quickly* get back behind the wheel and drive immediately at moderate speed to the nearest service station. You may have only a few minutes of driving before the radiator reheats and forces you to stop to let the engine cool.

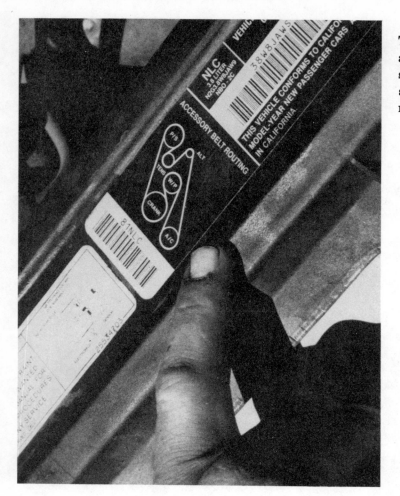

The hood diagram shows accessories powered by a serpentine belt—sometimes including the radiator fan.

THE CAR WON'T START OR STOPS IN HOT WEATHER

In sizzling hot weather, you're driving in bumper-to-bumper traffic. Without warning the engine quits. When you try to restart it, nothing happens. Your car may be afflicted with vapor lock—a hot-weather, hot-engine condition common during the summer.

Vapor lock is similar to another car malady, carburetor percolation, which also causes a hot engine to refuse to start once stopped. But while vapor lock happens while you're driving, carburetor percolation happens when, after a hot drive, you shut off the engine and can't restart it.

Both are caused by extreme engine heat under the hood. With vapor lock, heat causes the gasoline in the fuel line to bubble. The bubbles block the flow of fuel to the carburetor. With carburetor percolation, heat causes fuel in the carburetor's bowl to boil. Boiling over, it floods the engine. (Vapor lock and carburetor percolation don't affect late-model cars whose engines are fuel injected. They don't have carburetors to bubble, boil, or percolate.)

➤ WHAT TO DO

If the engine stops while you're driving in hot weather:

1. Don't continue to attempt to start it. If it's vapor-locked, you'll only run down the battery.
2. Get to the shoulder, perhaps by using the starter to inch there or with a push from a fellow motorist.
3. Raise the hood. Leave it raised. What the engine needs is cool air.
4. There is a simple way to hasten the engine's cooling and to "debubble" the gasoline in the fuel line and fuel filter, assuming you can locate them in the crowded engine compartment. The trick is to squirt water on the fuel line and filter to cool them and dissipate the gasoline-blocking bubbles.
5. The simplest solution, however, is to do nothing. Wait 30 minutes or so for the engine to cool. Then restart it.

If the engine won't start after you've shut it off in hot weather:

1. Open the hood to let the engine cool.
2. Wait to let it cool for 10 to 20 minutes.
3. Try to restart, while pressing the accelerator to the floor. It should start.

THE GAS PEDAL JAMS

Whether backed up in traffic or driving on a highway, if you ease your foot off the gas pedal and the car doesn't slow down, it may mean the gas pedal is stuck.

➤ **WHAT TO DO**

1. Brake fast and hard.
2. As you do, downshift to a lower, slower gear. The lower gear will help to brake the engine and your speed.
    Some experts advise switching off the ignition. While doing so "disconnects" the engine, slowing you, it also leaves most cars without power steering.
3. Quickly tap the gas pedal, momentarily depressing it in the hope it'll come unstuck.
4. If it doesn't, put a foot under the pedal and lift upward. Sometimes lifting the pedal unsticks it. On some cars, however, lifting the pedal disengages it from the throttle linkage, the mechanical connection between the pedal and the throttle under the hood.
5. If the engine is still revving at the speed you're stuck at, quickly reach down— keeping your eyes on the road—and lift the floor mat, if you have one, where it hugs or surrounds the gas pedal. Floor mats often cause gas pedal jams by snagging be- tween the floor and pedal, thus restricting the pedal's movement. If it's not the mat, something else—papers, discarded fast-food containers—may be causing the pedal to stick.
6. As hard braking slows you down, signal your intent to make for the shoulder. Get on the shoulder, brake to a stop, and switch off the engine. These quick corrective steps for handling, slowing, and stopping a car with a stuck accelerator may span no more than a minute or so.
7. When your nerves are steady, set the parking brake, put the transmission in Park or Neutral, and start the engine. Search the floor around the gas pedal, behind and be- neath it, for anything that might have impeded the pedal's movement. As you do, lift the pedal with your hand. If the pedal doesn't respond—doesn't return the engine to idle or moves sluggishly or hardly at all—you probably have a linkage problem.
    If you know where the throttle's linkage is under the hood, often a quick squirt

If the gas pedal sticks, quickly tap it to unstick it.

of a lubricant will unstick the pedal. Then again, the linkage may be bent. Either way, the problem demands a mechanic's attention.

8. Even so, you can usually drive off the highway to a repair shop if you do the following: turn on your warning flashers to let others know you have a problem. Stay in the lane nearest the shoulder or curb. Shift into a low, braking gear. Keep your foot on the brake pedal. Rein in the engine and your speed.

Keeping your eyes on the road, probe for a common cause of gas pedal jams: a floor mat stuck beneath the pedal.

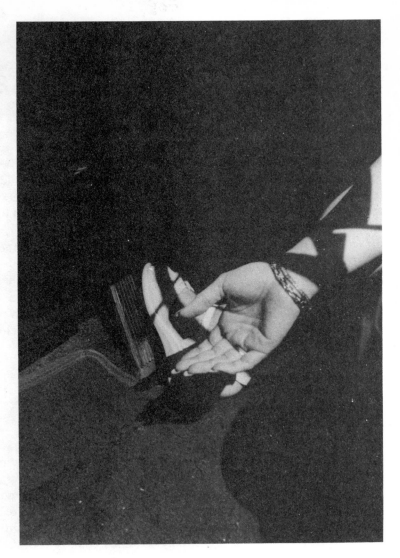

THE TRANSMISSION STICKS IN PARK

You park on a steep street or road shoulder, set the parking brake, shift the automatic transmission into Park, lock the car, and go about your business. When you return to the car, you find that you can't get the shift lever out of Park.

In the vexing minutes that follow, you may try everything, including: shutting the engine off and trying to shift again, revving the engine, releasing the foot brake, even consulting your owner's manual.

Your car may be "torque-locked." This can happen when a car (any transmission) is parked on a hill and, perhaps through no fault of the driver, the transmission is improperly put in Park. The force of the parking gear plus the car's weight can put too much force (torque) on the parking gear mechanism, particularly within a front-wheel-drive transaxle. The result is your transmission is locked in Park.

➤ **WHAT TO DO**

1. Do nothing to force the shift lever (you may possibly damage it as well as the transmission).
2. Short of trying to force the shift lever out of Park (in most cases, no reasonable use of force will budge it), try everything else that seems reasonable: try releasing the brakes; try shutting off the engine, restarting it and shifting it again; consult your owner's manual again (it may contain some tips for breaking the torque lock that is peculiar to your car and its transmission).
3. Apply the foot brake and, while holding it, try to shift out of Park. Some front-wheel drives have a brake-transaxle shift interlock. This prevents you from shifting out of Park when the ignition is on, unless the car's regular foot brake is fully applied as you attempt to shift.
4. It is also possible that you aren't properly or fully shifting, even though you believe you are. Still applying the regular brakes, push the shift lever all the way into Park. Continuing to apply the brakes, try shifting out of Park.
5. If all else fails, there *is* a remedy. While you keep a hand poised on the shift lever,

234

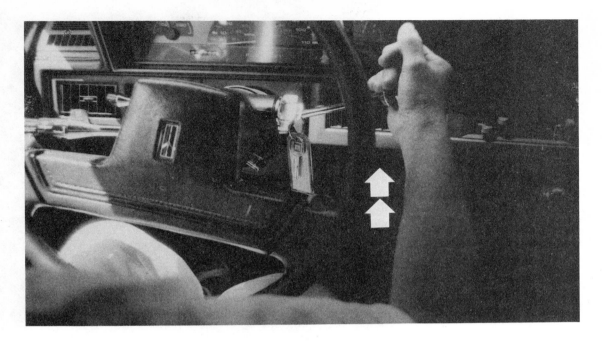

To unstick the transmission, try shifting fully into Park.

have a couple of friends (or another car) nudge you uphill a little. This should relieve the pressure on the transaxle and let you quickly shift out of Park, breaking the torque lock.

6. At the first opportunity, take the car to your dealer or to a mechanic for a consultation. While torque lock doesn't usually mean a transmission problem, there is always that possibility.

INDEX